BIG
ENGLISH 6

T0385912

Mario Herrera
Christopher Sol Cruz

PUPIL'S BOOK

Contents

CLIL	Writing	Life Skills/Project	Phonics	I can...
Social Science: School timetables in China daily, free time, period, study period, timetable, typical **Additional language:** *must* for obligation, *shall* for suggestions **A Day at a School in Finland:** An alternative school in Finland break, curriculum, objective, pace, task, workshop	Opinion paragraph	**Manage your time wisely.** Talk about how you spend your time and how you manage it. Create a graph to see how pupils spend their time.	**spr, str, scr** spring, sprint street, strong screen, screw	...talk about school activities and homework. ...say what I have and haven't done.
Social Science: Amazing accomplishments by young people through the ages accomplishment, ages, Braille, opera, personal computing, symphony **Additional language:** reflexive pronouns *whom* **Seeds of Peace:** The organisation for teens, *Seeds of Peace* conflict resolution, critical thinking, journalist, leader, peace	Biography	**Appreciate yourself.** Talk about your amazing qualities and talents. Make an 'Amazing Me' collage and interview classmates about their amazing qualities and talents.	**spl, squ, thr** splash, split squash, squid three, throat	...talk about past experiences. ...talk about amazing people's accomplishments (including my own).
Social Science: Ethics character, ethical behaviour, ethics, qualities, traits, treat **Proverbs from Around the World:** Proverbs in other cultures blame, deceive, pass on, proverb, regret, sayings	Story ending	**Do the right thing.** Discuss the right choice to make when faced with a dilemma. Make a class handbook about doing the right thing.	**nch, nth, mpt** crunch, lunch month, tenth prompt, tempt	...talk about consequences. ...talk about doing the right thing.
Science and Technology: Futurists' predictions in the areas of science and technology 3-D image, download, futurist, nano, upload, virtual, wireless technology **Kids' Predictions for the Future:** Predictions young people have made about the future environment, harmoniously, shelter, time machine, turn out	Formal and informal emails	**Make good decisions.** Talk about how the decisions you make now affect the future. Pupils write letters to themselves in the future and share them with the class.	**/s/, /z/, /iz/** eats, cooks, sleeps runs, sings, swims dances, washes, watches	...talk about and make predictions about the future. ...talk about levels of certainty.
Science: Scientific inventions that could allow humans to have super powers adhesive, computer designer, digital, electrodes, gecko, technology, tweet **Superheroes from Different Cultures:** Superheroes in different parts of the world android, armour, bolt of lightning, meteorite, reflexes, superhuman	Character traits	**Take positive steps for the future.** Discuss amazing achievements and things we can do to help the future of the world. Make a class book about positive steps for the future.	**/t/, /d/, /id/** looked, walked, watched called, cleaned, climbed ended, painted, wanted	...talk about what I would do in different situations. ...answer questions about unreal situations.
Science: Strange things found in nature algae, carnivore, digest, herbivore, nectar, nutrients, protein, sloth **Additional language:** complex noun phrases **Ancient Civilisations' Legacies:** The contributions of ancient civilisations cultivation, equivalent, herbal remedy, influence, inspiration, legacy, revolution, terraced farming	From story to play	**Appreciate school.** Complete a chart and discuss practical uses for the topics learnt at school. Create an album of words/names from ancient Greece that are used today.	**er, est** cheaper, easier, faster, happier best, longest	...talk about school subjects and what I learn. ...identify some legacies of ancient civilisations. ...compare things using *more/most*, *fewer/fewest*, *less/least*.
Science, Art, Music: The phenomenon of aurora borealis altitude, atmosphere, atoms, interaction, nitrogen, oxygen, solar winds, state **Additional language:** *whose* **Mysterious Findings:** Mysterious events in different parts of the world diameter, estimate, evidence, expedition, footprint, ton	Cause and effect	**Be curious.** Learn the importance of fostering one's own curiosity. Create a booklet about two mysteries.	**un, inter, re, pre, super** unhappy international recycle, reduce preused Superman	...discuss mysterious phenomena. ...confirm information using question tags.
History: Famous landmarks around the world that were discovered by accident archaeologist, artefact, carved, pharaoh, site, tomb **Additional language:** complex noun phrases **The New 7 World Wonders:** A bicycle trip to the new seven wonders of the world empire, gladiators, landmark, route, sea level	Report	**Take pride in your town or city.** Describe special places, monuments or other attractions of one's own town/city or a nearby city. Create a map for a bicycle trip to famous or interesting places in one's town/city.	**able, ful, ly** comfortable, washable beautiful, peaceful deeply, slowly	...talk about famous places and structures around the world. ...describe places and structures using the passive voice and relative clauses.
Social Science: The history of video games arcade, coins, compete, graphics, national, scores, shortage **Unique Musical Instruments:** Different musical instruments from around the world bagpipes, herdsmen, horn, mellow, notes, sitar, steel drums	Film review	**Appreciate different opinions.** Read and discuss the opinions of several young people. Make an opinion map to compare, discuss and record classmates' opinions about a topic.	**sion, tion, ation** decision, television fiction, option celebration, invitation	...talk about entertainment. ...talk about people's opinions. ...report what people say.

ALL ABOUT SCHOOL

1:04

1 Read and listen to the statements. All of them are true! Talk about them with a partner. Which one is the most surprising? Why?

1 Some kids have *didaskaleinophobia*, which is the fear of going to school.

2 Richard Branson, creator of *Virgin Records* and the *Virgin Atlantic* airline, didn't finish secondary school.

3 There is an alternative school in Canada that doesn't test pupils and it doesn't follow a strict timetable, either. Pupils decide how to spend the school day and which activities to attend. They are grouped not by their age but by their interests.

4 Finnish pupils rarely take exams or do homework until they are into their teens. But they rank at the top or near the top in international tests in Science, Maths and Language.

5 China's got the longest school day in the world. A Chinese pupil spends almost eleven hours in the classroom each day!

6 In South Korea, secondary school pupils applying for university all take the same standardised test. On the day of the test, people come to the school to support pupils who are going to take the test. They give out sweets, tea and other treats to the pupils. Some taxis give pupils free rides and additional trains and buses run before and after the exam.

1:05

2 Read and listen to these bad excuses. Say what each person should have done. Use the phrases in the box.

Use *should* + *have* + past participle form of the verb to give advice about something in the past.

been more careful   done it earlier
done it again   paid attention to the time
taken it away from her

1 Q: Have you done your homework yet?   She should have 🧩.

  A: No, I haven't…

2 Q: Have you studied for the test yet?   She should have 🧩.

  A: No, I haven't…

3 Q: Have you finished your project yet?   He should have 🧩.

  A: Yes, I have, but…

4 Q: Have you handed in your essay yet?   He should have 🧩.

  A: No, I haven't…

5 Q: Have you done your Maths homework yet?   He should have 🧩.

  A: No, I haven't…

3 Work with a partner. Take turns making up your own bad excuses.

Have you finished your homework yet?

Why not?

No, I haven't.

There was a power cut and I couldn't find my torch.

THINK BIG When do we usually give excuses? What's the difference between an excuse and an explanation?

4 Listen and read. What's the problem? What different advice is offered?

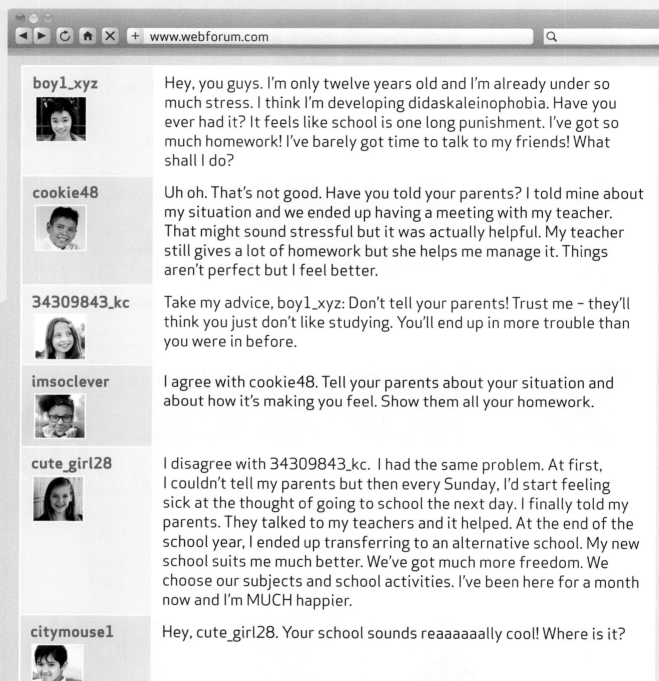

www.webforum.com

boy1_xyz
Hey, you guys. I'm only twelve years old and I'm already under so much stress. I think I'm developing didaskaleinophobia. Have you ever had it? It feels like school is one long punishment. I've got so much homework! I've barely got time to talk to my friends! What shall I do?

cookie48
Uh oh. That's not good. Have you told your parents? I told mine about my situation and we ended up having a meeting with my teacher. That might sound stressful but it was actually helpful. My teacher still gives a lot of homework but she helps me manage it. Things aren't perfect but I feel better.

34309843_kc
Take my advice, boy1_xyz: Don't tell your parents! Trust me – they'll think you just don't like studying. You'll end up in more trouble than you were in before.

imsoclever
I agree with cookie48. Tell your parents about your situation and about how it's making you feel. Show them all your homework.

cute_girl28
I disagree with 34309843_kc. I had the same problem. At first, I couldn't tell my parents but then every Sunday, I'd start feeling sick at the thought of going to school the next day. I finally told my parents. They talked to my teachers and it helped. At the end of the school year, I ended up transferring to an alternative school. My new school suits me much better. We've got much more freedom. We choose our subjects and school activities. I've been here for a month now and I'm MUCH happier.

citymouse1
Hey, cute_girl28. Your school sounds reaaaaaally cool! Where is it?

techieboy03

I've already researched alternative schools, citymouse1. There are some great ones in the UK. I've also researched similar schools in Scotland. There are some really cool ones that are unusual and interesting. I'm guessing but I think your school might be in London, cute_girl28. Am I right?

cute_girl28

You're close, techieboy03. Good guess! You're a great detective. There are a lot of alternative schools in London. I know because I researched it, too! My school is in Brighton. I just love my school!

boy1_xyz

I like your idea. I think an alternative school would fix my problem. But those schools are difficult to get into and there are only a few of them.

rainbowgirl

Why not try homeschooling? I'm being homeschooled and I really like it. My mum teaches me all the subjects. We go on field trips a lot. And once a year, we go to an event just for homeschoolers. It's very exciting. I look forward to it every summer!

READING COMPREHENSION

5 **Read and say** yes, no **or** doesn't say.

1 Boy1_xyz has already told his parents about his problem.

2 Cookie48 has spoken to his teacher about his problem.

3 Imsoclever and cookie48 give the same advice.

4 Cute_girl28 lives in Scotland.

5 Techieboy03 likes being at a traditional school.

THINK BIG Who do you think gave the best advice to boy1_xyz? Why/Why not? What advice would you give to boy1_xyz?

Language in Action

1:09

6 Listen and read. What have Peter and his mum already discussed?

Mum: Peter, I'm about to ask you a question. Can you guess what?

Peter: You're about to ask me if you can increase my pocket money.

Mum: Ha ha. Have you finished your homework yet?

Peter: Not exactly. I'm talking to Tessa.

Mum: Yes, I can see that. May I speak to you, please?

Peter: OK. *[to phone]* Tessa, I've got to go. I'll call you back later.

Mum: So you haven't 'exactly' finished your homework yet?

Peter: Yeah, well, I've finished my Maths homework and I've almost finished my English essay but I haven't started my History assignment yet.

Mum: We've been through this before, Peter. Homework first, phone calls later.

Peter: I know. Sorry, Mum. I'll do it now.

7 Practise the dialogue in **6** with a partner.

1:10

8 Listen and match. Then complete the sentences. Use the correct form of the verb.

> get his licence   meet the new pupil
> see the music video   walk the dog

a

b

c

d

1 Mark's brother has already 🔧.

2 Stacey hasn't 🔧 yet.

3 Roberto has already 🔧.

4 Dawn hasn't 🔧 yet.

Has she **done** her solo <u>yet</u>?	Yes, she **has**. She **has** <u>already</u> **done** it.
	No, she **hasn't**. She **hasn't done** it <u>yet</u>.
Have they <u>ever</u> **won** an award?	Yes, they **have**./No, they **haven't**.
Tip: Use the present perfect to talk about an event that happened at an indefinite time in the past. The specific time is unknown or unimportant.	

9 **Make questions and answers. Follow the example.**

1 **Q:** you/do/your homework/yet

<u>Have you done your homework yet?</u>

A: <u>Yes, I've already done it.</u>   **A:** <u>No, I haven't done it yet.</u>

2 **Q:** he/finish his project/yet

3 **Q:** they/ever/be on a field trip

4 **Q:** your parents/speak to the teacher/yet

5 **Q:** she/give the book back/yet

He **has** <u>already</u> **finished** the project.	He **finished** it <u>yesterday</u>.
He **hasn't finished** the project <u>yet</u>.	He **didn't finish** it <u>yesterday</u>.
Tip: Use the present perfect when no specific time is given. Use the past simple when giving a specific time in the past.	

10 **Look at Jan's to-do list. Then complete the questions about it and answer them. Follow the example.**

1 (*talk*) Has Jan <u>talked to Jenny yet?</u>
<u>Yes, she has. She talked to her at 4:00.</u>

2 (*check email*) Has Jan ❓

3 (*start reading*) Has Jan ❓

4 (*write essay*) Has Jan ❓

5 (*finish Science project*) Has Jan ❓

Things to do:

1 Call Jenny at 4:00. ✔
2 Check email at 4:15. ✔
3 Start reading my book. ✘
4 Write essay. ✔
5 Finish Science project. ✘

1:13

11 Listen and read. How much free time is there in a Chinese pupil's typical school day?

A Day in the Life of a Pupil in China

It's noon and the bell is ringing at your school. How many hours have you spent doing schoolwork by then?

Shall we take a look at a typical school day in China? Well the school day begins at 7:30 with a flag-raising ceremony and a speech from the head teacher. A pupil's daily timetable is packed. There is hardly any free time and pupils must work hard all day. Pupils, especially pupil leaders, have been trained from a young age to be good pupils, get good marks and help other pupils do the same. And school timetables show this. The school day is almost eleven hours long!

Look at a typical school timetable in China.

7:30–7:40 a.m.	flag-raising ceremony
7:40–7:45	prepare the classroom
7:45–8:30	1st period
8:40–9:25	2nd period
9:35–10:20	3rd period
10:30–11:00	morning exercises
11:10–11:15	eye exercises
11:25–12:10 p.m.	4th period
12:20–12:40	lunch
12:50–1:50	study period
2:00–2:15	free time
2:25–2:30	classroom prep
2:30–3:15	5th period
3:25–3:30	eye exercises
3:40–4:25	6th period
4:35–5:20	7th period
5:30–6:10	8th period or study period

12 Read 11 again and say true or false.

1 Chinese pupils prepare their classroom first thing in the morning.

2 Chinese pupils learn how to work hard and are usually good pupils.

3 A Chinese pupil's typical day at school is over twelve hours long.

13 Write your school timetable in a chart. Discuss it with a partner.

1:14

14 Listen and read. How do pupils at this school learn new things?

A Day at a School in Finland

"Moi, Sofia!" "Terve, Aleksi!" That's "hi" and "hello" in Finland. And that's how pupils and teachers greet each other at this Finnish school. Pupils call their teachers by their first names. Anna Hansson has gone to this school since Year 1 so she knows everybody. Anna shouts "Moi" to her fellow pupils as she arrives at 7:45 in the morning.

At her school, Anna and her classmates decide, along with their teacher, what their weekly objectives, tasks and activities will be. Pupils work at their own pace. They don't always study together. Some may be in their home classroom. Others might be in a workshop where they're learning by actually doing. Today, Anna's group is working on a magazine in a magazine workshop.

Anna and her classmates don't learn by memorising facts. Instead, they work together to gather information. They ask their teacher for help whenever they need to. At times, they even rest on the classroom sofa. The class is active and busy but the teacher is in full control and doesn't have to tell pupils to behave. Parents are welcome at the school and lend their expertise in workshops and evening classes.

After 90 minutes, pupils have a 30-minute break. Soon, it's lunchtime! At Anna's school, pupils get free hot meals every day. Today's lunch is everybody's favourite – meatballs and mashed potatoes. It is served with salad, bread and glasses of milk on tables with tablecloths and flowers in vases.

Chores have always been part of the curriculum at Anna's school. All pupils do chores, which include taking care of plants, collecting rubbish, recycling and composting. Pupils help in the library and in the kitchen.

School is over by 2 in the afternoon. Most parents work so in the afternoon, there are clubs and hobby groups. Pupils can study Japanese, learn to play instruments and do arts and crafts.

15 Read 14 **again and match.**

1 memorise facts   **a** research and record details

2 lend expertise   **b** learn and remember information

3 gather information   **c** share knowledge and skills

 THINK BIG How is Anna's school the same as your school? How is it different?

16 Read the opinion paragraph about homework.

Homework Does Not Make Pupils Learn Better

Does homework make pupils learn better? In my opinion, it does not. In fact, having a lot of homework makes pupils dislike school and become stressed. Pupils who are anxious and don't like school cannot learn well. Pupils who have got hours and hours of homework cannot relax and spend quality time with their families. I believe that school timetables should allow pupils to get most of their schoolwork done at school. In this way, when they get home, they can be free to enjoy time with their family or just relax. In my opinion, a more relaxed pupil will perform better in class. Too much homework prevents this!

17 Look at **16** again. Copy and complete the paragraph outline.

Title rewritten as question: 🔖
Main opinion: 🔖
Reason: 🔖
Suggestion: 🔖
Conclusion: 🔖

18 **Choose one of these school issues or use one of your own ideas and write about it:**
   - Do you think memorising facts makes pupils learn better?
   - Do you think school uniforms should be required?

1 Copy the chart in 17 and complete it with information about your topic.

2 Write your own paragraph.

3 Share it with the class.

19 How do you spend your time? Copy the list of activities and add two more. Tick (✔) the ones you have to do each week and write the number of hours.

Activity	Approximate hours per week
⑧ attend lessons	⑧
⑧ travel to and from school	⑧
⑧ eat	⑧
⑧ sleep	⑧
⑧ study or do homework	⑧
⑧ play sports or exercise	⑧
⑧ participate in school clubs	⑧
⑧ do chores	⑧
⑧ watch TV	⑧
⑧ chat with friends online or by phone	⑧
⑧ ⑧	⑧
⑧ ⑧	⑧

THINK BIG Do you think you manage your time wisely? Do you always have enough time to study, to take care of your health, to sleep and to relax? Are the activities you spend the most time doing important? Why/Why not?

PROJECT

20 Make a graph about how you spend your time in a typical school week. Share it with the class.

My graph shows that in a typical week, I spend most of my time at school or studying. But I also spend time with my friends, my family and on the phone and the internet. That's important! I don't spend enough time exercising. I'm going to work on managing my time better!

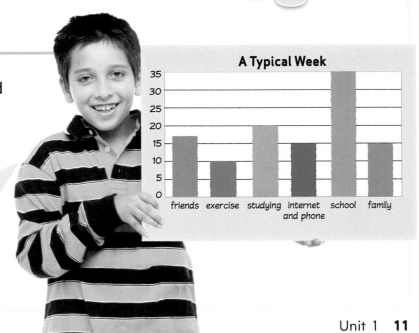

A Typical Week

Listening and Speaking

1:15

21 Listen, read and repeat.

1 spr   **2** str   **3** scr

1:16

22 Listen and blend the sounds.

1 spr-i-ng   spring   **2** str-ee-t   street

3 scr-ee-n   screen   **4** spr-i-n-t   sprint

5 str-o-ng   strong   **6** scr-ew   screw

1:17

23 Listen and chant.

I'm fast, I'm strong,
I can sprint all day long.
In the spring, in the street,
Greeting people that I meet!

24 Look at the list of school activities and think of some really bad excuses for why you haven't done these things yet. Work in a group. Ask and answer questions.

complete your research project   do your homework   join any after-school clubs
organise your backpack   write your book review

Have you done your homework yet?

No, I haven't. I lost my book on my way home!

No, I haven't. I started to do it but my dog ran off with it and ate it!

No, I haven't. I had to train his dog not to eat homework so I ran out of time!

1:18

25 Listen to Lucas and Nina talking about their school. What have they already done? What haven't they done yet? Copy the chart and put a tick (✔) or a cross (✘) next to the activities.

	Lucas	Nina
take the test		
hand in the research		
go to an art club meeting		
start the essay		

1:19

26 Listen again. Make sentences about 25. Follow the example.

1 take the test

Lucas hasn't taken the test yet.

Nina has already taken the test. She took it on Tuesday.

2 hand in the research

❓

3 go to an art club meeting

❓

4 start the essay

❓

I Can

- talk about school activities and homework.

- say what I have and haven't done.

AMAZING YOUNG PEOPLE

1:20

1 Most of us dream of doing great things during our lifetime. Read and listen to these popular life dreams. Which ones do you hope to achieve?

Dreams

- Climb Mount Everest
- Meet a world leader
- Ride a camel or an elephant
- Learn how to play the piano, the guitar or the violin
- Be a contestant on a game or reality show
- Take award-winning photos of nature
- Help the poor and those in need
- Speak another language or two
- Travel around the world
- Become a doctor and work in a developing country
- Start a company
- Become a millionaire
- Write and publish a book

2 Do a class survey. Find out which of the dreams in 1 are the three favourites.

3 Listen. You will hear about some amazing young people and what they've achieved. As you listen, find answers to the questions.

1 a When was Yifan born?

   b Where is she from?

   c What has she achieved?

> "I believe you should have goals and reach them step by step."
> *Hou Yifan*

2 a When was William born?

   b Where is he from?

   c What has he achieved?

> "With hard work, anything in life is possible."
> *William Kamkwamba*

3 a When was Johnny born?

   b Where is he from?

   c What has he achieved?

> "Pursue your dreams… Even if you don't succeed, if you try your hardest, the experience will help you…"
> *Johnny Strange*

4 Work with a partner. Talk about the people in 3.

Who do you think is the most amazing young person?

Johnny Strange. He's been climbing mountains since he was twelve!

THINK BIG How do you set and achieve your goals? Which of the people in 3 do you agree with the most? Why?

Unit 2 **15**

1:22

Listen and read. Why is Jimmy different from the kids around him?

JIMMY WOODARD:
COMPUTER WHIZZ-KID
by Chris Winger

Where do you see yourself at seventeen? Owning a business? Owning a car? Saving for university? Chances are you will eventually do these things but maybe not when you are seventeen... unless you are someone like Jimmy Woodard!

Jimmy Woodard is a high school pupil from Manchester, Vermont, USA. In many ways, Jimmy is a normal teenager who spends a lot of time online every day. But in other ways, Jimmy has always been different from the kids around him. When Jimmy was very young, his parents realised he had a special gift. While other children were playing with toys, Jimmy would take his toys apart to find out how they worked. But Jimmy's gift really became obvious when he started using computers. Jimmy was only six when he started using his parents' computer. That's not so unusual these days. However, in Jimmy's case, if he had a problem with the computer, he worked out how to fix it by himself!

When Jimmy was in the 5th year of primary school, his technology teacher gave him a computer to work on. Jimmy took the computer apart and put it back together again. Since then, Jimmy has been working with computers in his school, even helping teachers with their technology problems.

When he was fourteen, Jimmy decided to open his own technology consulting company. Since that time, he has brought in about 200 regular customers. One of them is former astronaut Gerald Carr. "It feels funny sometimes," said Jimmy with a smile. "I can't believe I'm helping an astronaut with his computer!"

Jimmy has done more than just work on computers. Since he was eleven or twelve, Jimmy has been helping and working in his community. He has managed the sound and lights for a local TV show and for theatrical performances. Jimmy has also worked as a DJ. "I've been a DJ at more than fifty dance events already," he said. "It's really fun."

Jimmy has saved a lot of money over the past three years. "I've just bought my own car," he said happily. "I've used some of my money to buy more computers or equipment for my company. But I'm trying to save the rest of it for university." As for his future, Jimmy explained, "I don't know what I want to do yet. I know I want to do something with computers. But I'm interested in a lot of different things. I'd like to live in a big city someday. I can't wait to see what happens next."

READING COMPREHENSION

6 Number the events in the order they happened in Jimmy's life.

a Jimmy rebuilt a computer.

b Jimmy bought a car.

c Jimmy started his own company.

d Jimmy took his toys apart to find out how they worked.

e Jimmy started using his parents' computer.

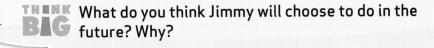

THINK BIG What do you think Jimmy will choose to do in the future? Why?

Language in Action

7 Listen and read. What has Zack been doing on the computer?

Mum: Zack, you've been on the computer for a while now.

Zack: I know. I've got to write a biography about an amazing person so I've been doing research on someone. This guy is so interesting!

Mum: Who is it?

Zack: William Kamkwamba. He's been a builder and an inventor since he was a teenager.

Mum: What has he built?

Zack: His village in Malawi had no electricity or running water. So he built a windmill. And he was only fourteen!

Mum: Wow. How did he know how to make a windmill?

Zack: He got some books from the library and studied the diagrams.

Mum: He made a windmill from a diagram? That's amazing!

Zack: I know!

8 Practise the dialogue in 7 with a partner.

9 Listen and complete the sentences.
Use the correct form of the verb.

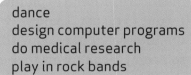

dance
design computer programs
do medical research
play in rock bands

1 She's _been dancing_ since _she was about five_ .

2 He's 🔊 for 🔊.

3 He's 🔊 for 🔊.

4 They've 🔊 together since 🔊.

How long **has** she **played** the piano?
She**'s played** the piano <u>for</u> five years.

How long **have** they **known** about William Kamkwamba?
They**'ve known** about him <u>since</u> they saw a film about him.

10 Read the information and then complete the sentences about each amazing person.
Use the present perfect and for or since.

> Hou Yifan is nineteen and a chess
> player. She started playing chess
> when she was three.

1 She ❓ chess ❓ sixteen years.

2 She ❓ chess ❓ she was three.

3 He ❓ mountains ❓ he was twelve.

4 He ❓ mountains ❓ ten years.

> Johnny Strange is twenty-two and a
> mountain climber. He started climbing
> when he was twelve.

How long **has** your brother **been playing** tennis?
He**'s been playing** tennis <u>since</u> he was five.

How long **have** you and your sister **been bungee jumping**?
We**'ve been bungee jumping** <u>for</u> two years.

11 Read the answers. Ask the questions. Use the present perfect continuous.

1 ❓

He's been saving money for university since he was thirteen.

2 ❓

We've been volunteering at the hospital for two years.

3 ❓

She's been filming her documentary since August.

4 ❓

I've been playing the piano since I was at nursery school.

5 ❓

They've been friends for seven years.

1:27

12 Listen and read. Who became an Olympic champion at the age of fourteen?

CONTENT WORDS		
accomplishment	ages	Braille
opera	personal computing	symphony

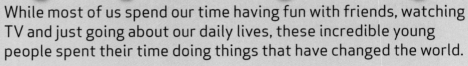

Amazing Young People Through the Ages

While most of us spend our time having fun with friends, watching TV and just going about our daily lives, these incredible young people spent their time doing things that have changed the world.

Read about some people who did amazing things when they were very young.

- Wolfgang Amadeus Mozart composed his first symphony by himself at eight and wrote an opera at fourteen.

- Louis Braille started working on his code for blind readers (later called Braille) when he was just twelve years old.

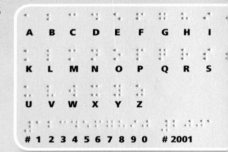

- Fourteen-year-old Nadia Comaneci scored a perfect 10 in gymnastics at the 1976 Olympic Games – an amazing accomplishment! She was the first person to achieve this!

- Pelé, whom every young footballer dreams about, was seventeen when he scored six goals in four games in a World Cup event, making Brazil the football champions that year.

- At nineteen, Steve Jobs started developing personal computing and Bill Gates co-founded a company called Microsoft.

- Also at nineteen, Mark Zuckerberg started Facebook, a social media website that has changed the way people around the world keep in touch with each other.

13 Copy and complete.

Who?	What?	Age?
Steve Jobs	❔	19
❔	work on code for blind readers	12
Mozart	write an opera	❔
Comaneci		14

1:28
14 Listen and read. What is 'Seeds of Peace'?

Seeds of Peace

Every day we hear about individuals, politicians and world leaders trying to bring peace to countries at war. But there's another group of people you probably haven't heard much about who are trying to do the same thing. And they're mainly teenagers. These teenagers belong to an organisation called Seeds of Peace.

Seeds of Peace was started in 1993 by a journalist named John Wallach. The group began with 46 teenagers and educators and has grown to over 5,000 participants in 27 different countries.

Each summer, 350 new 'Seeds' are carefully chosen by the group. This new group of teenagers attends the Seeds of Peace international summer camp, where they meet and live with other teenagers whose countries are 'enemy' countries. The campers learn important communication skills as well as conflict resolution and critical thinking skills. Most importantly, they learn how to make change happen.

Fifteen-year-old Sharon Koren summed up her expectations of the summer camp with these words: "My goal is to be as understanding as I can be, to be open to hear the other side and respect everyone. Everyone wants peace... I think we're going to make peace."

After the summer is over, these teenagers return to their home countries. They go home, not just with memories of new friendships but also with the idea that they can be leaders who can work together for a better future for themselves and for the whole world. They've learnt that the fighting around them doesn't have to go on forever.

15 Read 14 again and say true or false.

1 Seeds of Peace has thousands of participants.

2 Seeds of Peace members learn how to change things for the better.

3 Sharon Koren doesn't think there can be peace.

THINK BIG What do you think makes a person amazing? Why?

16 Read the biography.

My Brother Josh

My brother Josh is amazing! He was born in 1998 in Melbourne, Australia. Josh went to Melmoth Primary School there and was top of his class.

In 2008, my family moved to Bristol, in the UK. Josh has been very busy since we moved. He has played the drums with the school band, has been on the school football team and has joined the drama club.

Josh is really busy but he always takes time out to do things with me. That's what makes him so amazing!

17 Look at 16. Copy and complete the timeline about Josh.

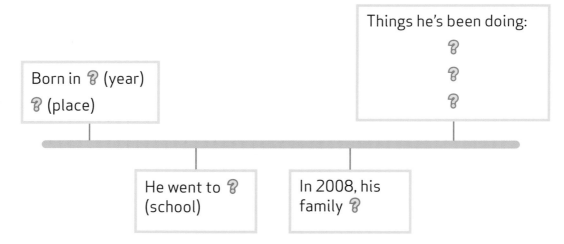

Things he's been doing:
❓
❓
❓

Born in ❓ (year)
❓ (place)

He went to ❓ (school)

In 2008, his family ❓

18 Write a short biography.

1 Interview an older relative or do research on an amazing person that you're interested in.

2 Create a timeline based on your interview or research.

3 Use your timeline to write the biography.

4 Share your biography with a partner. Discuss each other's work.

19 Just like the young people in this unit, all of us have amazing qualities and talents. Copy and complete a chart about you.

1 Think about your good qualities and talents.

2 Complete the first and second columns of the chart.

3 Ask a partner to name three things about you that are amazing.

4 Write them in the third column of the chart.

	My good qualities	What I'm good at	My classmate thinks I'm amazing because...
Ex.	I'm friendly.	playing the drums	I'm quite clever.
1.	𝔅	𝔅	𝔅
2.	𝔅	𝔅	𝔅
3.	𝔅	𝔅	𝔅

20 Now study your chart. Is your classmate's opinion of you the same as/different to your opinion about yourself?

AMAZING ME!

Family

DANCE

Creativity

PROJECT

21 Make an Amazing Me collage.

1 Include photos or drawings of yourself doing things you enjoy.

2 Include drawings, pictures from magazines and words and phrases that show who you are and what you like.

3 Write your name on the back and display your collage in the classroom.

22 Take turns guessing the person who made each collage. Then interview that person.

THINK BIG How can we make use of other people's opinions of us? Whose opinion counts the most?

Listening and Speaking

1:29

23 Listen, read and repeat.

1 spl   **2** squ   **3** thr

1:30

24 Listen and blend the sounds.

1 spl-a-sh	splash	**2** squ-i-d	squid
3 thr-ee	three	**4** spl-i-t	split
5 squ-a-sh	squash	**6** thr-oa-t	throat

1:31

25 Listen and chant.

> Take a dive in the deep blue sea.
> Splish! Splash!
> One squid, two whales
> And three dolphins, swimming free.

26 Work in a small group. Play a memory game. Follow the steps below.

> know   live   play   study   watch

1 Take turns making sentences with the verbs from the box. Follow the order shown. Here's an example:

Mary (Pupil 1): <u>I've known</u> Ben since I was six years old.

Tom (Pupil 2): Mary <u>has known</u> Ben since she was six years old. <u>I've lived</u> in Liverpool for ten years.

Anna (Pupil 3): Mary <u>has known</u> Ben since she was six years old. Tom <u>has lived</u> in Liverpool for ten years. <u>I've been playing</u> football since I was in Year 1.

2 Continue with the other verbs until a pupil can't remember all the sentences. Then start again with *know*.

Ed (Pupil 4): Mary <u>has known</u> Ben since… oh, no! I forget! Let's start again.

3 Talk about how you did as a group. Which pupil remembered the most sentences?

27 Complete the paragraph with for or since.

This is Jen and Ally. Jen has lived in Oxford **¹**  2008. Ally has been Jen's best friend **²** two years but they've known each other **³** Year 3. They like in-line skating but Jen hasn't done it **⁴** she was a little girl. Ally's teaching her how to do it again. They want to invite their friends to skate with them at the park. They've been talking about it **⁵** about a month! Maybe they'll go next weekend.

28 Complete the sentences. Use the present perfect continuous and for or since.

> have cooking lessons   play football
> practise the piano   sing opera

1 She ❓ she was six years old.

2 She ❓ the past eight years.

3 They ❓ Year 4.

4 He ❓ an hour.

I Can

• **talk about past experiences.**

• **talk about amazing people's accomplishments (including my own).**

unit 3 DILEMMAS

1:32
1 Listen and read. What would you do? Work with a group to choose an answer for each situation. Then compare and discuss answers with another group.

Your older sister is supposed to be home by 10:00 p.m. One night, you see your sister leave at 9:00. At 10:00, your sister still isn't home. You're worried about her but if you tell your parents, your sister will get into trouble. And she might be just a few minutes late. But something might be wrong!

Answer 1: You should tell your parents right away.
Answer 2: You should wait an hour before you tell them. Everything is probably OK.

Two classmates have found the answer key to a Maths test near the photocopier. You see them pick it up and hear them talking about it. They tell you that they'll show you the answers if you don't tell anyone. You're not doing well in Maths. You really need to pass this test. If you look at the answers and cheat in the test, you'll feel guilty and dishonest but you'll pass. If you tell the teacher about the answer key, the boys will be angry and you probably won't pass.

Answer 1: You should talk to the boys and tell them to put the answer key back or you'll tell the teacher.
Answer 2: You should look at the answer key and not tell the teacher.
Answer 3: You should just tell the boys you're not interested and walk away.

2 You'll hear three people talking about dilemmas or difficult situations they've experienced. Listen. Then read about their concerns.

Dilemma #1

> If I keep the wallet, I'll feel guilty.

Emily

Dilemma #2

> If I tell my friend I lost her necklace, she'll be upset with me.

Angela

Dilemma #3

> If I confess I broke the lamp, I'll get into trouble.

Al

3 What's the right thing to do? Think of advice to give to Emily, Angela and Al. Then listen and compare your answers.

1 Emily, I think you should 🐾.

2 Angela, I think you should 🐾.

3 Al, I think you should 🐾.

4 Work with a partner. Talk about the dilemmas. Use the expressions in the box or your own ideas.

> be upset with (him/her)
> feel good
> feel guilty
> get into trouble

> What will happen if Emily returns the wallet?

> If she returns the wallet, she'll feel good! And the man will, too!

THINK BIG How do you cope with dilemmas? Who do you discuss them with? Why?

1:35 5 Listen and read. What's Marissa's dilemma?

MARISSA MOBLEY'S
DILEMMA

by Milan Norman

Marissa Mobley walked into the kitchen and said, "I'm home." She didn't sound happy. Mrs Mobley looked at Marissa.

"Is something wrong?" she asked. "You don't sound happy."

"Oh, nothing, Mum," Marissa replied. "I've just got a lot of homework."

Mrs Mobley looked worried. "Are you sure you're OK?" she asked again.

"Umm… yeah, Mum. I've just been doing too much at school lately. So I'm tired. That's all," Marissa said as she walked into her room and closed the door.

Marissa's brother, Leo, knocked on Marissa's door. "Hey, what's up?" asked Leo. "Something's wrong. I can see it in your face."

"Well," said Marissa, finally, "can you keep a secret? I've got a problem at school. It's a real dilemma. You know Dan, right?"

"Dan? Yeah, I know him," said Leo. "He's a funny guy."

"Well, I don't think he's so funny. At least not this week," Marissa said. "Listen to this. He asked me to help him cheat in our Maths test on Friday."

"What?" Leo asked.

"I guess Dan's marks in Maths aren't very good this term," said Marissa. "If he doesn't do well in the test, he won't be able to play for the basketball team any more. He sits next to me in Maths and he knows I do well in tests. He wants me to make it easy for him to see my paper during the test."

"Seriously?" said Leo. "That's not good."

"I know," said Marissa, sounding more and more upset. "I've been thinking about it all week and it's bothering me a lot. I'd like to help Dan but helping him cheat really isn't helping him! I just can't do it!"

"Of course you can't!" her brother said. "If a boy asks you to help him cheat in a test, you should tell your teacher!"

"Tell my teacher? If I do that, Dan will get into *big* trouble," said Marissa.

"But if you help him cheat, you'll be cheating, too, Marissa," said Leo.

Marissa sighed. After a minute, she smiled and looked at her brother. "I know!" she said.

"What are you going to do?" Leo asked.

"Wait and see," Marissa answered. Then she picked up her mobile phone.

READING COMPREHENSION

 Find one detail in the story that supports these statements.

1 Marissa's mum knows Marissa isn't happy.

2 Marissa doesn't tell her mum the truth about her problem.

3 Marissa trusts her brother Leo.

4 Leo doesn't want Marissa to help Dan cheat.

5 Marissa doesn't think telling the teacher is a good idea.

6 Marissa's got an idea about what to do.

 THINK BIG Why do you think Marissa has been having a hard time deciding what to do? What do you think she's going to do next? Why?

Language in Action

7 **Listen and read. What should Chris do?**

Ashley: This is fun! Can we play *Lost World 3* next?

Chris: Uh, no. We can't. The disc is broken.

Ashley: Broken? How'd that happen?

Chris: I was running to catch the bus and I dropped it. Before I could pick it up, someone stepped on it.

Ashley: Oh, no. Did you tell Sam? He's going to be upset.

Chris: No, I haven't told him yet. I was hoping he would forget that I borrowed it from him.

Ashley: But you've got to tell him! He won't be upset if you replace it. You can buy him a new disc with your pocket money.

Chris: You're right. I'll buy him a new one and tell him what happened.

8 **Practise the dialogue in 7 with a partner.**

1:38

9 **Listen and complete the sentences.**

1 If she tells the truth, ?.

2 If she keeps it, ?.

3 If he goes to the concert, ?.

4 If he doesn't tell his mum what's wrong, ?.

> **If** he **pays attention** in class, he**'ll understand** the lesson.
>
> **If** they **don't study** for the Maths test, they **won't get** a good mark.
>
> **If** you **tell** me the truth, I**'ll help** you.

> **Tip:** Use a conditional sentence to express true or factual ideas in the present or future.

10 **Complete the sentences. What will they do?**

1 If my older brother wants me to lie for him, (I / not do) 🤔 it.

2 If Sarah says bad things about Michelle, (I / change) 🤔 the subject.

3 If you help me with my book review, (I / help) 🤔 you with your project.

4 If you tell Mum we lent Anna her CD, (she / be) 🤔 upset.

5 (I / not read) 🤔 my sister's diary if I see it on her desk.

> You **should tell** your parents **if** you've got a problem at school.
>
> **If** you don't want to get into trouble, you **shouldn't lie**.

11 **Which is the best advice? Make sentences with** should **or** shouldn't.

1 You see someone being bullied.

  a Just walk away.   **ⓑ** Tell an adult.

2 You tear an expensive shirt in the changing room in a shop.

  a Quietly return it to the rack.   **b** Tell a shop assistant what happened.

3 Your brother's going to watch a film that he's not allowed to see.

  a Tell your parents about it.   **b** Don't say anything to your parents.

4 Your sister's studying and you want to listen to music.

  a Tell her to go to a friend's house.   **b** Use headphones.

5 Your friend asks you to let him copy your English homework.

  a Tell your teacher.   **b** Offer to help him do his homework.

1:40

12 **Listen and read. What does 'ethics' mean?**

> **CONTENT WORDS**
> character   ethical behaviour   ethics   qualities   traits   treat

Ethics

The saying 'Treat others the way you'd want them to treat you' is not hard to understand. It means that you should behave towards others the way you'd want them to behave towards you. It sounds simple but is not always simple to do. If everyone did this, the world would be a much better place.

This unit is about ethics and ethical behaviour. Do you know what 'ethics' means? Of course you do. You make choices based on ethics all the time. Ethics tells you what's right or wrong, fair or unfair, acceptable or unacceptable. Choosing to do the right thing is ethical behaviour.

The word *ethics* comes from the Greek word *ethos*, which means 'character'. Our character – all of our traits and qualities taken together – is what leads us to do what we do – right or wrong. What kind of 'character' have you got? Are you respectful of your classmates? That's a question of ethics. Would you cheat in a test to make sure you pass? That's a question of ethics. Would you tell a 'harmless' lie in order to avoid hurting someone's feelings? That's also a question of ethics. Would you lie to someone to get out of trouble? That's a question of ethics, too.

Tips for Deciding What's Right

If you're not sure about what to do, ask yourself these questions:

1 If I do it, will I feel bad afterwards?

2 Could doing it cause anybody harm?

3 How would I judge someone else who did the same thing?

4 What would my mum or dad say about it?

And most importantly…

5 What's my gut feeling about it?

13 **Read 12 again and say true or false.**

1 Treating others the way you'd want them to treat you is very easy to do.

2 If you choose to do the wrong thing, then you're an 'ethical' person.

3 Trusting your gut feelings will help you decide what's right.

1:42
14 Listen and read. What's a proverb?

Proverbs from Around the World

Every culture's got its own proverbs. *Proverbs* are short sayings about life that are passed on from generation to generation. Proverbs provide sound advice and can help us make decisions. Across cultures, proverbs can be similar but some are quite different. Here are a few of the thousands of proverbs from around the world.

Country	Proverb
Argentina	If you have a tail of straw, stay away from the fire.
China	One step in the wrong direction can cause a thousand years of regret.
Germany	A clear conscience is a soft pillow.
Greece	Avoid doing what you would blame others for doing.
Ireland	A friend's eye is a good mirror.
Italy	Deceive me once, shame on you; deceive me twice, shame on me.
Liberia	Do not look where you fell but where you slipped.
Malaysia	Don't think there are no crocodiles just because the water is calm.
Mexico	Better to be alone than be in bad company.
Netherlands	He who has a choice has trouble.
Russia	You can get to the ends of the world on a lie but you cannot return.

 15 Read 14 again and find the country.

1 You'll sleep well if you don't feel guilty.

2 Having no friends is better than having a bad friend.

3 Don't give anyone a second chance.

 THINK BIG Choose three different proverbs and explain what they mean.
Research three more proverbs about ethical behaviour.
Discuss their meaning and present them to the class.

16 Work with a partner. Answer questions about 'Marissa Mobley's Dilemma' (see pages 28–29).

1   Who are the characters in 'Marissa Mobley's Dilemma'?

2   How does Marissa feel when she gets home from school?

3   Who knocks on Marissa's door?

4   What's Marissa's dilemma?

5   What advice does Marissa's brother give her?

6   At the end of the story on page 29, what do you think Marissa is going to do?

17 How do you think the story ends? Discuss these possible endings with a partner. Think of a reason why each one is possible.

* Marissa helps Dan cheat.

  Reason: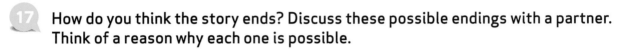

* Marissa tells her teacher about Dan.

  Reason:

* Marissa tells Dan she can't help him.

  Reason:

* Marissa helps Dan study.

  Reason:

18 With your partner, write an ending to the story. Add details, such as how the other story characters react to Marissa's decision and how she feels about it.

19 Share your story ending with another pair. Discuss. Talk about what Marissa did and whether it was the right thing to do.

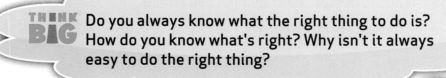

THINK BIG Do you always know what the right thing to do is? How do you know what's right? Why isn't it always easy to do the right thing?

20 Read about three situations and three possible courses of action for each one. Which one is the right thing to do? Discuss with a partner.

Situation	#1	#2	#3
You're getting into your mum's car. You see an envelope full of money on the ground.	Tell your mum about it and ask if you can keep the money.	Pick up the money quietly but don't tell your mum about it.	Tell your mum and ask her how you can return the money.
Your teacher gives you the highest mark for your book review and uses it as a model for the rest of the class. Your older sister wrote the book review for you.	Do nothing. Be happy and accept the mark and the compliment.	Tell your teacher you didn't write the review and apologise.	Tell your parents what you did but don't tell your teacher.
Your teacher goes out of the room during a big test. Your classmate, who's the best pupil in the class, tries to show you her answers.	Copy your classmate's answers – after all, she offered. It'd be silly to say no.	Compare your answers with hers but change only a few to match hers.	Tell your classmate, "No, thank you".

PROJECT

21 Make a page to go in a class handbook about doing the right thing.

1 Choose a dilemma from the unit or use one of your own. Describe it at the top of the page.

2 Write three possible courses of action.

3 Use a picture from a magazine or draw one to show the right thing to do.

4 Present your page to the class. Read it aloud. Then say what you think the right thing to do is.

5 Bind the pages together to make a class handbook.

> I think she should run after the man and return the tablet to him. If she doesn't, she'll feel terrible later.

Dilemma: You're at a park. You see a man sitting on a bench with a tablet. He leaves the park and you notice he's left his tablet on the bench. You've always wanted one but you haven't got enough money to buy one. What should you do?

1: Sit on the bench and cover the tablet so no one sees it.

2: Don't say anything but hold onto the tablet in case the man comes back for it. Secretly hope he doesn't!

3: Run after the man and return the tablet to him.

Listening and Speaking

1:43

22 Listen, read and repeat.

1 nch   **2** nth   **3** mpt

1:44

23 Listen and blend the sounds.

1 l-u-nch   lunch   **2** t-e-nth   tenth

3 p-r-o-mpt   prompt   **4** c-r-u-nch   crunch

5 m-o-nth   month   **6** t-e-mpt   tempt

1:45

24 Listen and chant.

I make lunch
On the tenth of the month.
An apple and crisps.
Do you want any sweets?
Don't tempt me!
Crunch! Crunch!

Packed lunch

25 Work in groups of three. Choose a situation from the box or create your own. Pupils 1 and 2 role play the situation. Pupil 3 states the right thing to do.

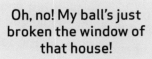

Oh, no! My ball's just broken the window of that house!

If you break something, you should tell the owner.

You should go up to the front door and talk to the owner.

You:
- lose your friend's CD.
- see someone cheat in a test.
- spill juice on your friend's new shirt.
- see a man drop his wallet.
- break your friend's mobile phone.
- are asked to lie for your brother/sister.
- break a window at home.
- forget mother's day.

26 Complete the sentences with expressions from the box.

> | be upset with | feel good about |
> | feel guilty (3x) | get into trouble |

1 Claudia saw a man drop his wallet. When she picked it up, she saw that there was a lot of money in it. She was tempted to keep it but she knew it wasn't right. She thought about what to do. By the time she decided to return the man's wallet, he was gone. Claudia 🔲. She 🔲 herself for not deciding quickly enough.

2 Anna saw two classmates looking at each other's papers during an exam. She didn't know what to do. She knew it was wrong to cheat but she didn't want her friends to 🔲. Anna 🔲 about not saying anything.

3 Mike was at a toy shop and was holding a robot when he accidentally broke it. He didn't have the money to pay for the toy so he put it back on the shelf and quickly left the shop. Michael 🔲. He didn't 🔲 what he did.

 27 Read the problems in 26 again. Choose one. In your notebook, write what you think the person should have done.

 28 Complete the sentences with the correct form of the verb in brackets and will.

1 (tease) I 🔲 be kind to my friend if others 🔲 him.

2 (ask) If my friend 🔲 me to help her cheat, I 🔲 not do it.

3 (get) I 🔲 spend my money carefully if I 🔲 some from my grandparents.

4 (promise) If I 🔲 to do something, I 🔲 do it!

5 (spend) If you 🔲 all your pocket money, I 🔲 lend you some of mine.

6 (spill) If I 🔲 juice on the sofa, Mum 🔲 be very upset with me.

I Can

● **talk about consequences.**   ● **talk about doing the right thing.**

How Well Do I Know It? Can I Use It?

1 Think about it. Read and draw. Practise.

😊 I know this.　　😐 I need more practice.　　☹ I don't know this.

	PAGES			
School Activities: study for a test, hand in an essay, finish a project…	3	😊	😐	☹
Advice: be more careful, do it again…	3	😊	😐	☹
Achievements: climb a mountain, start a company…	14–15	😊	😐	☹
Dilemmas: (tell/don't tell) the truth, (return/don't return) a wallet, (cheat/don't cheat) in a test…	26–27	😊	😐	☹
Results and Consequences: feel good, feel guilty, get into trouble…	27	😊	😐	☹
Has he **practised** his part <u>yet</u>? Yes, he **has**. He**'s** <u>already</u> **practised** his part. No, he **hasn't**. He **hasn't practised** it <u>yet</u>. **Have** the twins <u>ever</u> **studied** abroad? Yes, they **have**. / No, they **haven't**.	6–7	😊	😐	☹
How long **has** he **played** the guitar? He**'s played** the guitar <u>for</u> five years. How long **has** she **been playing** in a band? She**'s been playing** in a band <u>since</u> she was fourteen.	18–19	😊	😐	☹
If he **studies** hard for the Maths test, he**'ll get** a good mark.	30–31	😊	😐	☹
You **should talk** to your parents about it.	30–31	😊	😐	☹

1:46

2 Get ready.

A Choose the correct word or phrase to complete the dialogue. Then listen and check.

Mum:	The school play is tomorrow night. Have you (learnt / learning) your lines yet?
Danny:	I've (learn / learnt) most of them already. We've been (practised / practising) for two weeks.
Mum:	Really? I didn't (know / known) that. Where have you (practise / been practising)?
Danny:	We've (practising / been practising) every day at school, after lunch.
Mum:	And have you (studied / studying) for your Maths test tomorrow?
Danny:	Yeah, I've (studied / studying) a bit.
Mum:	You should (study / studying) again after dinner tonight.
Danny:	But Mum, I need to (practise / practising) my lines for the play! If I (forget / forgot) my lines on stage, I'll (feel / feeling) awful.
Mum:	I know, Danny, but if you don't (pass / passing) your Maths test, you'll (feel / felt) even more awful and then you won't enjoy your play! Listen – study Maths for an hour, then you can practise your lines again for an hour. You should (try / will try) to get a good night's sleep, too.
Danny:	OK, Mum. Thanks.

B Practise the dialogue in **A** with a partner.

C Ask and answer the questions with a partner.

1 Has Danny studied enough for his Maths test? Explain.

2 Why does Danny's mum want him to get a good night's sleep?

3 Which do you think Danny should do first, study for his test or learn his lines? Explain.

4 Have you ever had to do two important things at one time? What happened?

Get set.

 STEP 1 Cut out the cards on page 121 of your Activity Book.

 STEP 2 Lay out all the cards on your desk. Now you're ready to **Go!**

 Go!

A Work with a partner. Look at the questions. You will use them to create two dialogues.

B Create the first dialogue. Pupil A reads these questions and Pupil B chooses five responses from the cutouts. Read the dialogue aloud.

C Switch roles and create the second dialogue. The new Pupil A reads these questions and the new Pupil B answers the questions with the remaining cutouts.

Pupil A
1 Have you chosen the topic of your project yet?
2 Why did you choose that topic?
3 What do you need to do for the project?
4 Have you already started the project?
5 Do you need to buy anything for the project?

D Now make up your own dialogue. Role play your dialogue in front of another pair.

Pupil A	**Pupil B**
You're the mum or dad of Pupil B. You want to know all about your son or daughter's project.	You're doing a project on a topic that you're really interested in. You've already started the project but you haven't finished yet.

5 Write about yourself in your notebook.

- How long have you been learning English?
- What kinds of things have you liked best about your English lessons?
- If you learn English well, what will you be able to do in the future?

All About Me

Date: _____

_____

_____

How Well Do I Know It Now?

6 Look at page 38 and your notebook. Draw again.

A   Use a different colour.

B   Read and think.

I can start the next unit.

I can ask my teacher for help and then start the next unit.

I can practise and then start the next unit.

7 Rate this Checkpoint.

 very easy   easy   hard   very hard   fun   OK   not fun

1

2

3

4

5

6

7

8

9

DREAMS FOR THE FUTURE

2:07

1 Read the predictions made by John E. Watkins in the year 1900. Say which predictions you think came true. Then listen to check.

I, John E. Watkins, an American civil engineer, predict that in one hundred years from now…

1 Trains will travel at speeds of up to 240 kilometres per hour.

2 A man in the middle of the Atlantic Ocean will be talking to his family in Chicago. It'll be like his family is sitting next to him!

3 People will be buying ready-cooked meals.

4 People will be sending photographs from anywhere in the world. Photographs of major events from another continent will be in newspapers in an hour and they'll have the colours of nature.

5 People will be eating strawberries as big as apples! Raspberries and blackberries will also be big.

6 Americans will be taller by three to five centimetres.

2 Look at the list as you listen to two boys discussing their dreams for the future. Which topics do you hear them talking about?

DREAMS FOR THE FUTURE

I'll be working in my dream job.

I'll be running my own business.

I'll be living in another country.

I'll be married.

I'll be bringing up a family.

I'll be working in the music industry.

I'll be going on adventurous holidays.

I'll be speaking several foreign languages including English.

I'll be earning a good salary.

I'll be famous.

3 Imagine your life in twenty years. Look at the list in 2 and think about each statement. Which do you think you'll be doing?

4 Work with a partner. Ask and answer about what you'll be doing in twenty years.

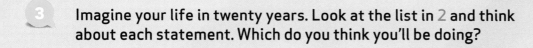
What will you be doing in twenty years?

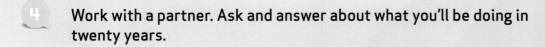
I'll be working in the music industry and earning a good salary.

 THINK BIG What do you think the world will be like thirty years from now in terms of:
- education?
- transport?
- everyday life?

2:03

5 On futureme.org, people write to themselves in the future. MeToday has written three emails to her future self. Listen and read. How old will she be ten years from now?

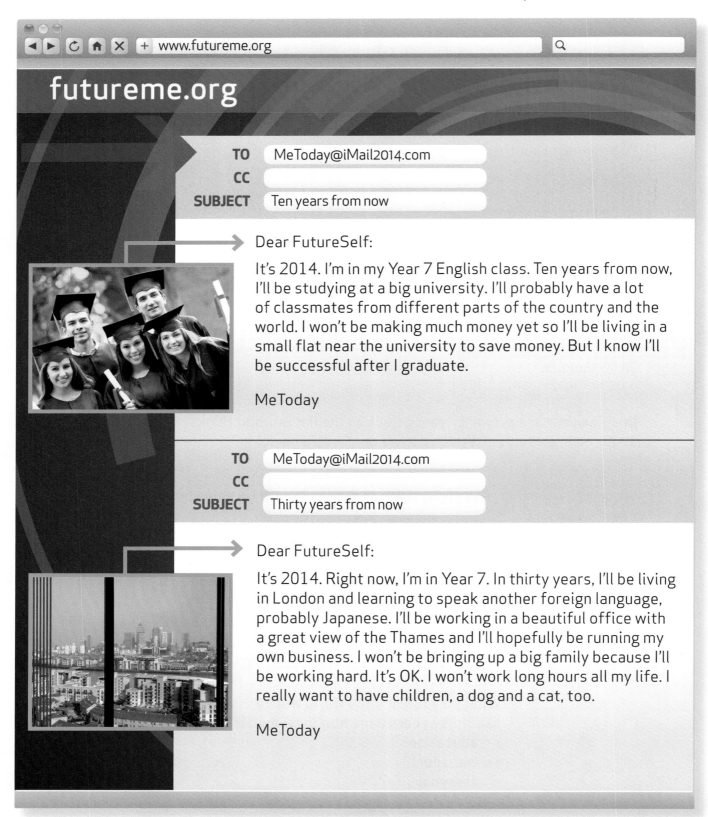

futureme.org

www.futureme.org

TO MeToday@iMail2014.com
CC
SUBJECT Ten years from now

Dear FutureSelf:

It's 2014. I'm in my Year 7 English class. Ten years from now, I'll be studying at a big university. I'll probably have a lot of classmates from different parts of the country and the world. I won't be making much money yet so I'll be living in a small flat near the university to save money. But I know I'll be successful after I graduate.

MeToday

TO MeToday@iMail2014.com
CC
SUBJECT Thirty years from now

Dear FutureSelf:

It's 2014. Right now, I'm in Year 7. In thirty years, I'll be living in London and learning to speak another foreign language, probably Japanese. I'll be working in a beautiful office with a great view of the Thames and I'll hopefully be running my own business. I won't be bringing up a big family because I'll be working hard. It's OK. I won't work long hours all my life. I really want to have children, a dog and a cat, too.

MeToday

www.futureme.org

TO MeToday@iMail2014.com

CC

SUBJECT Fifty years from now

Dear FutureSelf:

It's 2014. I'm twelve years old this year and I'm in Year 7. Wow, I'll be sixty-two years old fifty years from now! I'll probably be living back home in my country. I definitely won't be working. I'll be living in a small house, enjoying my retirement. My grandchildren will be visiting me often. We'll be taking rides in my flying sports car!

MeToday

READING COMPREHENSION

 What will MeToday be doing in the future? Find and compare with a partner.

1 Find two things MeToday will be doing ten years from now.

Find one thing she won't be doing.

2 Find two things MeToday will be doing thirty years from now.

Find one thing she won't be doing.

3 Find two things MeToday will be doing fifty years from now.

Find one thing she won't be doing.

THINK BIG Is there anything about MeToday that you admire? Explain.
Do you think MeToday will be successful? Why/Why not?

Language in Action

2:05

7 Listen and read. Where will people be going on holiday in the future?

Lisa: I'll definitely buy a nice car when I grow up.

Gavin: A car? We'll probably be flying around in spaceships when we're older!

Lisa: You're such a dreamer.

Gavin: Well, maybe in <u>twenty or thirty</u> years.

Lisa: So, do you think we'll be taking a spaceship to work every day?

Gavin: Why not? I'll be living in <u>Tokyo</u> and working in <u>Madrid</u>.

Lisa: But the world is running out of oil. If there's no oil, how will we fly around in spaceships?

Gavin: People will discover a new source of fuel so we won't need oil.

Lisa: But if we've all got spaceships, travelling won't be exciting any more! Where will we go on holiday?

Gavin: Maybe we'll be <u>visiting other planets</u>!

8 Practise the dialogue in 7 with a partner. Change the underlined words.

2:06

9 Listen and match. Then complete the sentences. Use the correct form of the verb.

1 In 100 years, we'll 🔋.

2 In twenty years, she'll 🔋.

3 In fifteen years, he'll 🔋.

4 In forty years, they'll 🔋.

> live in
> read
> travel to
> work on

a

b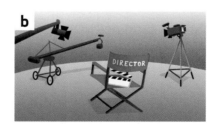

c

d

What **will** you **be doing** ten years from now?	I'll definitely **be studying** at a big university.
Where **will** you **be living** in twenty years?	I probably **won't be living** in Europe.

Tip: Use the future continuous to talk about what you'll be doing in the future. For degrees of certainty (how likely something is), use either *definitely* or *probably*.

10 What will you or won't you be doing forty years from now? Make complete sentences. Use the future continuous of the verbs in brackets and definitely or probably.

1 (live in another country) ?

2 (run my own business) ?

3 (go on holidays on the moon) ?

4 (go on white-water rafting trips) ?

5 (teach chemistry at the university) ?

6 (make a big archaeological discovery) ?

Will you **be running** a business?	No, definitely not. I definitely **won't**...
	Yes, definitely. I definitely **will**...
	Probably not. I probably **won't**...
	Yes, probably. I probably **will**...

11 Make Yes/No questions about the future. Use the ideas below or your own ideas. Exchange your questions with a partner. Take turns with your partner to ask and answer your questions.

bring up a family

make huge scientific discoveries

live in a big city

earn good money

travel around the globe

make a difference to the world

work for an environmental organisation

act in films/on TV

2:08

12 Listen and read. How will we be learning new skills in the future?

CONTENT WORDS

3-D image	download	futurist	nano
upload	virtual	wireless technology	

EXPERTS' PREDICTIONS FOR THE FUTURE

Futurists are people whose job is to look ahead and help us plan for the future. Here are a few of their predictions for the next fifty years.

Virtual Reality

In a virtual-reality game, you, as a player, experience an imaginary world and interact with the game characters as though you were part of that world. Now, imagine yourself in a virtual-reality school of the future where you would be socialising and learning with virtual people. Cool, don't you think? In order for this to happen, a 3-D image linked to your brain will make you feel as though you were actually in the classroom and interacting with your virtual teacher and virtual classmates.

Nanotechnology

Nanotechnology is the science of incredibly small things. Exactly how big is a nano? *Nano* means 'billionth', so a nanometre is one billionth of a metre! When something is nano size, it's so small, it's invisible! With nanotechnology, we'll have microscopic computerised robots called nanobots! Because nanobots can be built into almost anything – even appliances – household chores will be easier.

Brain-to-Computer Communication

How about this for an amazing prediction: One day, everyone and everything will be linked through wireless technology. Nanocomputers will be in your system so your brain, just like a computer, will be receiving downloads and uploads. Do you want to learn a new language or how to tango? As soon as you think the thought, your brain will be uploading the new language and the dance steps and you'll be learning them instantly!

 13 Read 12 again and say true or false.

In the future,

1 ...you'll be able to 'go to school' without leaving home.

2 ...nanobots will only help us with household chores.

3 ...you'll be able to learn a new language in no time.

 THINK BIG If you could learn something instantly by uploading it to your brain, what would you like to learn? Why? Do you think learning like this would be a good thing?

2:10

14 Listen and read. How many predictions are there about technology?

Kids' Predictions for the Future

When it comes to predicting the future, look no further than your classmates! Why? In the world of predictions for the future, kids have had some amazing ideas. In some cases, their predictions, especially about technology, have turned out to be true or most likely will be coming true. Here's what some kids from around the world have predicted for the future:

People around the world will be living happily. They will accept and help each other. Everyone will have food and shelter. People will be enjoying life because they'll have time.

People, no matter what their skin colour, gender, culture or religion, will be co-existing harmoniously together. The environment will be safe to live in.

In the future, there will be more space travel. There may be people living on Mars or on the moon.

Nanobots and nanopets will be living with us. We won't have to do anything. Our nanobots will be doing our work for us. For example, they can go shopping for us. They can even entertain us.

There will be a time machine that can show us what we'll look like in the future. We can also use the time machine to show us the past – like what our parents and grandparents looked like when they were young.

15 **Read 14 again and match.**

1 shelter
2 harmoniously
3 gender
4 co-existing

a female or male
b a safe place to live
c living together
d in peace

16 With a partner, read these two emails and decide which is formal and which is informal. Discuss the differences with your partner.

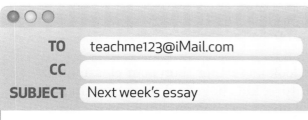

TO teachme123@iMail.com
CC
SUBJECT Next week's essay

Dear Ms Priscott,
I'll be working on next week's essay this weekend because I've got play rehearsals all week but I need more information about it. I've got some questions:
- What type of essay will we be writing?
- I'm planning to write about future technology. Is this topic OK?
- What is the deadline for the essay?
Thank you for your help.
Thomas Brown

TO howcoolisit1@iMail.com
CC
SUBJECT This weekend

Hey Leo,
Any plans 4 tomorrow? Wanna hang out at my house? I'm staying home all day coz ive got to babysit my little sister. Wanna do homework together?
Got the new video game, btw. It's brilliant!
Just text me b4 u come over. OK? CU soon.
Thomas

17 Write two emails: one to a teacher and one to a friend.

Formal

TO
CC
SUBJECT

Dear _____

Informal

TO
CC
SUBJECT

Hey _____

THINK BIG How can thinking about the past help you make better decisions in the present? Do you think it's good or bad to be thinking about and making plans for the future? Why/Why not?

18 Many young people don't think too much about the future. But they should. Read these statements. Think of a response to each one.

> Why do I have to learn English? I don't plan on living abroad so I don't need it.

?

> My parents own a business. I don't need to finish school because I'll be running the business when I'm old enough.

?

> Me? Learn how to do household chores? I don't think so! I'll have maids at home so I won't be doing any chores in the future.

?

PROJECT

19 Make a FutureSelf book. Write a letter to yourself fifteen, thirty, even fifty years from now! Make a class book.

Dear FutureSelf,

Today is 4th January, 2014 and I'm in Year 7. Fifteen years from now, I'll be living on a tropical island. I'll be teaching at a school there and living near the beach. I won't be married or have children yet. I'll be...

2:11

20 Listen, read and repeat.

1 eat**s**   **2** sing**s**   **3** wash**es**

2:12

21 Listen and blend the sounds.

1 c-oo-k-s   cooks   **2** r-u-n-s   runs

3 w-a-tch-es   watches   **4** s-l-ee-p-s   sleeps

5 s-w-i-m-s   swims   **6** d-a-n-c-es   dances

2:13

22 Listen and chant.

> Sol swims in the summer,
> He cooks in the winter,
> He dances on Fridays,
> He sings in the shower
> And he sleeps for hours!

23 Create class surveys.

1 Work in groups. Brainstorm a list of predictions.

2 Choose a group leader. The group leader conducts a class survey about one of your predictions.

> Will you be working in the fashion industry in thirty years?

> Yeah, I probably will be. I'm interested in designing clothes and I love art.

3 As a group, add up the results and create a graph. Then present your graph to the class.

> In our class, 15 out of 30 pupils think they definitely won't be working in the fashion industry.

Working in the Fashion Industry

24 Use the words in the box to complete the expressions.

> a business   a family   a foreign language
> a good salary   adventurous holidays   children
> in a dream job   in a nice office   in another country

1 run ?

2 work ?

3 earn ?

4 bring up ?

5 go on ?

6 speak ?

25 In your notebook, write four sentences about what four of your classmates will be doing in the future. You can use the expressions in 24 plus probably or definitely.

26 In your notebook, write answers to the questions. Use complete sentences.

1 What will you probably be doing tonight at 7:20?

2 What will you be doing this time next year?

3 Will you be travelling with friends ten years from now? Why/Why not?

4 What will you definitely not be doing in the future?

5 Will you be bringing up a family fifteen years from now?

6 What will you be doing forty years from now?

7 Will you be earning a lot of money twenty years from now?

8 Will you be travelling in space fifty years from now?

I Can

- **talk about and make predictions about the future.**

- **talk about levels of certainty.**

IF I COULD FLY...

1 Listen and read about ideas that could change our lives. Discuss the questions in small groups. Then share your favourite idea with the class.

Now You See Me – Now You Don't!

In the Harry Potter films, Harry puts on a cloak that makes him invisible. When he does that, nobody can see him! Have you ever wished that you could be invisible? If so, you may get your wish sooner than you think. Scientists have been working on bending light around objects to make them hard to see. Think about it. If you could become invisible, what would you do?

Time After Time

People have always thought about travelling to a different time period. What about you? Would you like to go back to mediaeval times and meet a real knight? Or would you like to see what the future will be like in 100 years? Maybe someday you'll be able to do this! If you could travel through time, what time period and place would you visit? Why?

It's a Bird! It's a Plane! It's a... Car?

Did you know that flying cars already exist? This vehicle's got four wheels and wings that fold up. You can drive it on the road. And you can also open up the wings and fly in the air! Would you like to have a flying car? What would you use it for?

2 Some pupils are talking about things they could do if they had one of the super powers in the box. Listen and match.

2:15

superhuman strength	the ability to become invisible
the ability to fly	the ability to read people's minds
the ability to run at lightning speed	the ability to travel through time

If you could have one super power, what would it be?

If I had this super power...

1

I know what super power I'd want!

2

There are so many things I could do...

3

I think I'd choose...

4

I'd want to have...

5

3 Work with a partner. Talk about super powers.

If you could have one super power, what would it be?

I'd want the ability to read people's minds.

THINK BIG What other super powers can you think of that could be useful to people? Do you think any of them could become reality? Why/Why not?

2:16
4 Listen and read. What's wrong with Captain Allsafe?

CAPTAIN ALLSAFE TO THE RESCUE!

by Buster Marone

READING COMPREHENSION

5 Number the events from the story in the order they happened.

   a Captain Allsafe ties up a 'dinosaur'.

   b Captain Allsafe sees a 'fire' and blows it out.

   c Captain Allsafe sees smoke. He throws water and puts out the 'fire', pouring water onto the barbecue!

   d Captain Allsafe is flying over the city and everything seems calm and quiet.

   e Captain Allsafe hears children screaming.

   f Captain Allsafe says that maybe he should go on a holiday.

   g A woman brings out a birthday cake.

THINK BIG Why doesn't Captain Allsafe want to go on holiday? If you were Captain Allsafe, would you go on holiday? Why? If you could give Captain Allsafe some advice, what would you tell him?

Language in Action

2:18

6 Listen and read. What would Ben and Alexa do if they had a certain super power?

Ben: I'm reading about this guy who can make objects move just by thinking about them. Isn't that cool?

Alexa: That's very cool. I wish I could do that.

Ben: Yeah? If you could move things with your mind, what would you do?

Alexa: I'd clean up my room – hands-free, no physical effort.

Ben: You're thinking too small, Alexa. If I had that power, I'd move our town closer to the beach.

Alexa: Oh! I like that. Then we could move all our friends' houses next to our houses.

Ben: Now you're getting the idea.

7 Practise the dialogue in 6 with a partner.

2:19

8 Listen and match. What would each person do? Make complete sentences.

go back in time	have any job
have anything to eat	talk to animals

1 If Maya could 👂, she'd 👂.

2 If Kelly could 👂, she'd 👂.

3 If Luke could 👂, he'd 👂.

4 If Daniel could 👂, he'd 👂.

if clause	result clause
If I **were** you,	**I'd choose** something else.
If he **made** his bed every day,	his mum **would be** happy.
If she **could have** one super power,	she**'d breathe** underwater.

Tip: Use *if* to talk about situations that are not true or contrary to fact. For example: *If I were you = I'm not you.*

9 Choose the correct verbs to complete the sentences.

1 If I (could breathe / would breathe) underwater, I (will explore / would explore) the bottom of the sea.

2 If I (owned / will own) a horse, I (would ride / will ride) it every day.

3 If you (ate / will eat) healthier food, you (are going to be / would be) stronger.

4 If we (can read / could read) people's minds, we (knew / would know) when they were lying.

If you **didn't have to go** to school, what **would** you **do** every day?	If I **didn't have to go** to school, I **would stay** home and **listen** to music all day.
If you **could go** anywhere, where **would** you **go**?	If I **could go** anywhere, **I'd go** to Paris.

10 Choose phrases from the box to complete the questions. Then answer the questions for you. Make complete sentences.

> who would you like to meet?
> whose mind would you read?
> when would you travel to?
> where else would you be now?
> what would you dream about?

1 If you could be in two places at the same time, 🔖

Answer: 🔖

2 If you could meet a TV or film star, 🔖

Answer: 🔖

3 If you could make up your own dreams, 🔖

Answer: 🔖

4 If you could read people's minds, 🔖

Answer: 🔖

5 If you could travel through time, 🔖

Answer: 🔖

2:21

11 Listen and read. Which idea involves a computer reading your mind?

CONTENT WORDS

adhesive   computer designer   digital   electrodes   gecko   technology   tweet

Super Power...
or Science?

Can scientists invent super powers? Read about ways in which humans are able to do things beyond what we think of as human abilities.

Wall Climbing

Have you ever seen a gecko climb up a wall and wondered why it didn't fall off? Geckos have got very sticky feet which keep them from slipping off the wall. If a human could climb like a gecko, it would seem like a super power. Scientists are experimenting with plastic to make an adhesive (a kind of glue) that will let humans climb up walls and they are close to working it out!

Think and Tweet

How would you like to be able to tweet without using a keyboard? Believe it or not, there's a scientist who's trying to make this possible! His experiment involves wearing a cap with electrodes. While wearing the cap, he concentrates on one letter at a time, spelling out his message on a computer screen – slowly! He's able to tweet eight letters a minute. But in the future, who knows?

All Digital, All the Time

Mark Rolston, a computer designer, thinks that computers, as we know them – a monitor, a keyboard, speakers – limit us. He believes that digital technology should be available to us everywhere. For example, in your kitchen, you should be able to watch the news on the kitchen table, make a video phone call on your refrigerator and read a recipe on the wall above your cooker. Would you like that?

12 Read 11 again and say true, false or doesn't say.

1 It's very possible that humans will soon be able to climb up walls.

2 Scientists are hopeful that soon they'll be able to 'think and tweet' a hundred letters a minute.

3 According to Mark Rolston, there are only a few things that digital technology can do for us at present.

2:23

13 Listen and read. Which hero comes from a country that is an island?

SUPERHEROES FROM DIFFERENT CULTURES

Superheroes come with all kinds of talents and abilities. And they come from all over the world. Take a look at some of them!

Superhero name:
Cat Girl Nuku Nuku

Everyday name: Atsuko 'Nuku Nuku' Natsume

Everyday occupation:
Pupil

Country of origin: Japan

Powers:
- is a highly advanced android
- has got the reflexes and senses of a cat
- has got superhuman strength

Superhero name:
Bantul the Great

Everyday name:
Bantul

Everyday occupation:
Various odd jobs

Country of origin: India

Powers:
- is extraordinarily strong
- can move big things by blowing air from his mouth
- has got hair so tough that each strand is like a thorn

Superhero name:
Meteorix

Everyday name:
Aldo

Everyday occupation:
Pupil

Country of origin: Mexico

Powers:
- has got superhuman strength
- can throw bolts of blue lightning
- can cover himself with blue armour by swallowing a meteorite

14 Read 13 again. Which hero or heroes...

1 can move very heavy things?

2 is like a cat?

3 can eat hard stone from outer space?

4 has got thick, strong hair?

THINK BIG Do you know any other superheroes? What are some of their powers and special skills?
Why do you think people like to read stories about superheroes?

15 Create and describe a superhero character of your own. Use the questions to help you. Take notes and discuss with a partner.

- What are your character's superhero and everyday names?
- What is his or her everyday occupation?
- What is his or her country of origin?
- In what time period does your character live?
- What does he or she look like?
- Has he or she got a family? If so, describe each member.
- What are your character's super powers?
- What is your character's mission?

16 Use your answers in 15 to copy and make a card about your character in your notebook. Draw a picture.

Superhero name:

Everyday name:

Everyday occupation:

Country of origin:

Time period:

Description:

Family:

Super powers:

Mission:

17 Swap and talk about your superhero cards. Which ones do you like best?

18 In real life, no one has super powers. But there have been some super achievements. Discuss them with a partner and decide which three are the greatest.

We have…

1 visited the moon.

2 invented alphabets and writing.

3 invented hot-air balloons and aeroplanes.

4 mapped the stars.

5 found ways to prevent and cure many diseases.

6 learnt how to use electricity.

7 created systems that bring clean water into homes.

8 invented the internet.

19 Make a list of three positive steps you could take to help with the future of our world. Discuss them with a partner and choose the best one.

> If I could do three things to help improve the world, I would…

THINK BIG Why is it important to think about the future of the world now? What can you do to help people start thinking about our world's future?

> If I could do one thing, I'd help clean up our oceans and seas!

20 Create a page for a class book about positive steps for the future. Share your page with the class.

1 Create a page for your best positive step for the future from 19.

2 Draw pictures or use pictures from magazines to illustrate it.

3 Show your page and talk about why the step is important.

Protect Our Oceans

Oceans make up 70% of our Earth

Listening and Speaking

2:24

21 Listen, read and repeat.

1 walked   **2** cleaned   **3** painted

2:25

22 Listen and blend the sounds.

1 w-a-tch-ed   watched   **2** cl-i-mb-ed   climbed
3 w-a-n-t-ed   wanted   **4** l-oo-k-ed   looked
5 c-a-ll-ed   called   **6** e-n-d-ed   ended

2:26

23 Listen and chant.

> We walked in the jungle
> And we climbed trees
> Which ended in the sky!
> We looked at birds
> And we wanted to fly!

24 Conduct an interview.

act in a film with any actor	become invisible
have any kind of pet	live anywhere
move things with your mind	sing with any musician or band
travel anywhere in the world	

1 Choose a classmate to interview.

2 Ask him/her questions using the ideas in the box. Note down their answers.

If you could travel anywhere in the world, where would you go?

I'd go to Argentina. I'd love to see the penguins!

If he could travel anywhere in the world, he'd go to Argentina to see the penguins.

25 Complete the sentences with the correct phrases from the box.

| be invisible | fly | have superhuman strength |
| read my mind | run at lightning speed | travel through time |

1 If you could ❓, you'd know what I'm thinking right now.
2 I wish I could ❓ right now. I don't want anyone to see me.
3 In the film, the hero ❓ so he lifted the car off the railway track.
4 In the story, the character could go back to the past. He could ❓.
5 He's a gold medallist in athletics. He can practically ❓!
6 If we could ❓, we wouldn't need to spend money on plane tickets!

26 Complete the sentences using the words or phrases in brackets and your own information.

1 (fly)
   If I ❓, I ❓.

2 (read people's minds)
   If I ❓, I ❓.

3 (become invisible)
   If I ❓, I ❓.

4 (be a scientist)
   If I ❓, I ❓.

5 (have superhuman strength)
   If I ❓, I ❓.

6 (be older)
   If I ❓, I ❓.

7 (run at lightning speed)
   If I ❓, I ❓.

8 (meet someone from the past)
   If I ❓, I ❓.

9 (travel to the future)
   If I ❓, I ❓.

10 (be a famous person for a day)
   If I ❓, I ❓.

I Can

- **talk about what I would do in different situations.**
- **answer questions about unreal situations.**

unit 6 THE COOLEST SCHOOL SUBJECTS

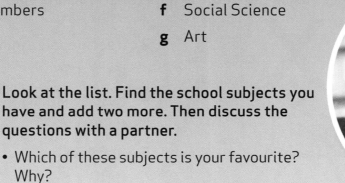

2:27

1 Read. Match what you learn to the school subject where you learn it. Listen to check.

Things we learn about		School subject	
1	Shakespeare	a	Maths
2	democracy	b	P.E.
3	sloths and pitcher plants	c	English
4	sports and athletics	d	Literature
5	vocabulary and grammar	e	Science: Biology
6	prime numbers	f	Social Science
7	murals	g	Art

2 Look at the list. Find the school subjects you have and add two more. Then discuss the questions with a partner.

- Which of these subjects is your favourite? Why?
- Name some things you learn about in this subject.
- Which subject is the most difficult for you? Why?

Maths	P.E.
English	Science
Social Science	Art
Literature	?

2:28

3 Listen. A group of pupils is putting on a game show. Copy the chart and complete it as you listen.

| artist | democracy | mammal | meat-eating plant |
| Olympic Games | playwright | prime numbers | speakers of English |

	What each question is about	**School subject**
1	the earliest ?	?
2	the greatest ?	?
3	the earliest form of ?	?
4	the ten smallest ?	?
5	the slowest ?	?
6	the biggest ?	?
7	the most ?	?
8	Mexico's greatest mural ?	?

4 Have your own game show! Work in small groups. Follow the steps.

1 Choose your roles: Assign a game show host and contestants.

2 The host should use his/her notes from the chart above to ask the contestants questions.

3 See who gets the most correct answers.

4 Having fun? Take turns being the host. Use other information from your own lessons to ask more questions.

This is a Social Science question. Ready? Where were the earliest Olympic Games held?

They were held in Greece!

THINK BIG Which three school subjects do you think are the most important? Why?

2:29
5 Listen and read. What decision did Paris have to make?

The Judgment of Paris

A GREEK MYTH
retold by *Sam Riley*

Once upon a time, the Greek goddesses Hera, Aphrodite and Athena were arguing about who among the three of them was the fairest – or the most beautiful – goddess on Mount Olympus. They needed some help so they chose Paris, the youngest son of King Priam of Troy, to be the judge. Of course, it wasn't a very objective process. All three goddesses offered Paris the best gift they could offer in order to make Paris decide in their favour. Athena, the Greek goddess of wisdom and knowledge, offered Paris wisdom; Hera, the wife of Zeus, offered him power. But in Paris's mind, Aphrodite, the goddess of love and beauty, gave the best offer of all: she would give Paris the most beautiful woman in the world. So Paris made his decision: The fairest goddess on Mount Olympus was Aphrodite. He gave her a golden apple which had this inscription: 'To the fairest'.

But Aphrodite didn't tell Paris that there was a problem with her offer. As it turned out, the most beautiful woman in the world wasn't free. Helen, Queen of Sparta, was the most beautiful woman in the world at the time and King Menelaus was her husband. But a promise is a promise. Besides, Aphrodite was the goddess of love; with her power, she could make anyone fall in love.

So Aphrodite sent Paris to Sparta, where King Menelaus and Queen Helen welcomed him. Aphrodite kept her promise. She made Helen fall in love with Paris and the two ran away to Troy, where Paris lived. King Menelaus was, of course, furious. He asked all the best Greek warriors to help him get Helen back. In response, more than a thousand Greek ships and a hundred thousand Greek soldiers set sail for Troy. And that was how the Trojan War began.

READING COMPREHENSION

6 **What did the goddesses offer to Paris to make him judge in their favour?**

1 Athena

2 Hera

3 Aphrodite

7 **Answer the questions.**

1 Whose offer did Paris accept?

2 What was the problem with Aphrodite's offer?

3 How did Aphrodite keep her promise to Paris?

4 How did the Trojan war begin?

 THINK BIG If you were Paris, would you agree to be the judge of this contest? Why/Why not? Whose gift would you accept? Why? What does Paris' choice show about him as a person?

Language in Action

Listen and read. What is Angela going to do for her Literature assignment?

Dad: Hi, Angela. You look happy. It seems like you've been enjoying school these days.

Angela: I have been. We've been reading a lot of Greek myths and legends in my Literature class. They're really great.

Dad: This may surprise you but I love myths and legends, too.

Angela: Do you? Well, maybe you can give me some advice. Our teacher wants us to write a play based on a myth.

Dad: That sounds like fun. How about 'Pandora's Box'?

Angela: I know that one. Pandora opens a beautiful clay box that she wasn't supposed to open and evil escapes into the world. That one's a little depressing.

Dad: Good point. Maybe you could do 'The Judgment of Paris'.

Angela: Hmm... that sounds familiar. What's it about?

Dad: I'll tell you the story...

9 **Practise the dialogue in 8 with a partner.**

Listen and match. Then complete the sentences. Include most or least and an adjective from the box.

> amazing   difficult
> endangered   favourite

1 He's looking for the ? of the play.   2 You can do the ? with these!

3 This is one of the ? in the world.   4 This is her ? in the school year.

a

b

c

d

China's got **more** speakers of English **than** the USA.

I've got **fewer** school subjects **than** my brother.

Teachers in Finland give **less** homework **than** teachers in the UK.

Tip: Use *fewer* with countable things. Use *less* with amounts that aren't countable.

11 **Complete these facts about plants and animals. Use** more, fewer **and** less.

1 Sloths spend 🔮 time doing any form of activity than most animals. Most of their time is spent sleeping or just hanging out – upside down!

2 There are 🔮 fish than dogs and cats as pets in the UK. There are approximately 40 million fish in tanks and ponds and 17 million pet dogs and cats in the UK.

3 The panda spends 🔮 time sleeping than eating. Pandas eat bamboo for 14 to 16 hours a day!

4 Trees use carbon dioxide to make food. The 🔮 trees there are, the 🔮 carbon dioxide in the atmosphere.

The Amazon rainforest has got **the most** species of plants and animals on Earth.

Germany and Switzerland have got **the fewest** pet dogs per capita.

Which country has got **the least** amount of air pollution?

12 **Complete the text with** the fewest, the least **or** the most.

Antarctica is full of extremes. It is ¹🔮 remote region on Earth. There are no permanent residents. This makes Antarctica ²🔮 populated continent on the planet. In spite of the snowy conditions, Antarctica is actually considered a desert. It's got ³🔮 amount of rainfall of any place in the world. Not surprisingly, Antarctica has got ⁴🔮 flowering plants of any other continent. The McMurdo Dry Valleys, one of ⁵🔮 extreme desert regions in the world, is the largest ice-free region in Antarctica.

2:35

13 Listen and read. What do you think is the strangest thing about sloths?

> **CONTENT WORDS**
>
> algae   carnivore   digest   herbivore
> nectar   nutrients   protein   sloth

Biology: The Weirdest Living Things

The Slowest Animal in the World

Sloths are the slowest animals on Earth. It takes them a month to move one kilometre! Sloths are also one of the sleepiest animals alive. They sleep up to twenty hours a day! They barely move at all, even when they're awake. They are so slow moving that algae grow on their fur! Everything they do is slow: they eat slowly, blink slowly and move slowly.

Sloths live in trees and eat only leaves and fruit. They eat, sleep and give birth upside down in trees.

The Largest Meat-Eating Plant

The pitcher plant is the largest meat-eating plant in the world. It's so big that it can even digest rats.

How do pitcher plants get and digest food? The plant's sweet-smelling sticky nectar attracts insects and small animals such as rodents. The cup-shaped plant has got slippery sides with small ridges that point downward towards the base, making it an excellent trap for the insects and other animals it eats.

However, the pitcher plant doesn't actually 'eat' food the way animals do. The plant's nectar contains chemicals similar to those found in our stomachs. These chemicals break down the protein and other nutrients in the meat until they can be absorbed by the plant.

> ## TIP
> Knowing the meaning of parts of words can help you work out the meaning of a word.
> **carni** = flesh
> **herbi** = herb or grass
> **vore** = swallow

14 Read 13 again and answer the questions.

1 Are sloths herbivores or carnivores?

2 Why can't insects that get into a pitcher plant climb out?

3 Are pitcher plants herbivores or carnivores?

15 Listen and read. Which ancient civilisation influenced our modern culture the most?

History: Legacies of Ancient Civilisations

Ancient Greek Civilisation

Of all the ancient civilisations, the ancient Greeks have had the most influence on modern culture – in the arts, in politics and government, in sports and in almost every aspect of our life and culture. Here are some examples:

- Ancient Greece gave the world its fascinating myths and legends, which have been rich sources of inspiration for films and plays.
- Athletes and sports fans can thank the Greeks for the first Olympic Games, which took place in the Greek city of Olympia in 776 BC.
- Perhaps the Greeks' biggest contribution to modern culture was the concept of democracy. The word *democracy* comes from the Greek word *demokratia* – *demos* meaning 'people' and *kratos* meaning 'rule'.

Ancient Aztec, Mayan and Incan Civilisations

Like the ancient Greeks, the ancient American peoples also left us legacies, or gifts. The Aztecs developed a number system based on 20. They are also known for advancing the cultivation of cacao, a key ingredient in chocolate.

The Maya developed a 365-day calendar system by observing Earth's revolution around the sun. They also introduced the equivalent of the Arabic zero (0).

Finally, the Inca introduced terraced farming, which is still practised today. The medical field also has the Inca to thank for the use of herbal remedies to treat illnesses.

16 Read 15 again and say Greeks, Aztecs, Maya or Inca.

1 They developed a system for calculating time.

2 They developed an advanced political system.

3 They knew how to cultivate cocoa.

4 They developed a way of farming that is still used today.

THINK BIG What other legacies from these or other ancient civilisations do you know about? Research and share with a partner.

17 Read the fairy tale. Note down anything a character thinks, wonders, wishes or says.

The Ugly Duckling

A mother duck sat on her nest. One of her eggs was much larger than the others. She wondered why the egg was so big. Soon the egg hatched. Out came a very big and odd-looking duckling.

"PEEP!" said the big duckling and blinked.

"Go away!" the duckling's brother snapped. He told the duckling that he was the ugliest duckling he'd ever seen.

The poor duckling didn't know what to do so he ran away. Autumn came and went and soon winter chilled the air. The duckling shivered, cold and alone.

Finally, spring came and the duckling stretched his neck down to the water to drink. He saw a beautiful bird reflected in the water. He wished he could look like the bird in the reflection. "Then people wouldn't call me an ugly duckling," he said.

A little girl throwing bread to him heard what the duckling said. "But that *is* you!" she cried. "You're not an ugly duckling – you're a swan!"

18 Rewrite the story as a play. Complete it in your notebooks. Then read it aloud to a partner.

Narrator: Mother Duck looks at her eggs.

Mother Duck: *[to herself]* 🔖

Narrator: The egg hatches. Out comes the Ugly Duckling.

Ugly Duckling: 🔖

Ugly Duckling's brother: 🔖

Narrator: The Ugly Duckling runs away. Autumn and winter come and go. Spring arrives. The Ugly Duckling looks down at the water and sees something.

Ugly Duckling: *[to himself]* 🔖

Little Girl: 🔖

19 Work with a partner. Find a fairy tale. In your notebook, rewrite it as a play. Read your play aloud to the class.

20 The subjects you learn at school have practical and important uses in everyday life. Can you think of a practical use for each of your subjects? Copy and complete the chart.

School subject	Topic learnt	Everyday use
Literature	Myths and legends	help us recognise our faults; teach us valuable lessons about life and people
Maths		
Social Science		
Science		
Art and Music		
Health and P.E.		
English		

PROJECT

21 Work with a group. Make a book of names from ancient Greece that we use today.

1 Write the Greek name and say what it stood for.

2 Draw a picture.

3 Share your page. Explain why it's a good name to use today.

The Amazons were female Greek warriors. They were brave and strong. There's a company with this name that sells products online. The name makes people think that the company is strong.

Amazon

THINK BIG Which is your least favourite school subject? Why? What can you do to learn to appreciate the knowledge it offers you?

2:39

22 Listen, read and repeat.

1 er   **2** est

2:40

23 Listen and blend the sounds.

1 f-a-s-t-er   faster   **2** ea-s-i-er   easier

3 b-e-s-t   best   **4** ch-ea-p-er   cheaper

5 h-a-pp-i-er   happier   **6** l-o-n-g-e-s-t   longest

2:41

24 Listen and chant.

> Running is faster than walking,
> Walking is cheaper than driving,
> Driving is easier than flying,
> Flying is harder than cycling,
> Cycling is the best!

25 Make a sentence using the words in each row of the chart.

Pupil	Adjective	Activity
1 Hannah	most	has got books in her backpack
2 Robert	fewest	has got coins in his pockets
3 Cheryl	most	has got songs on her mp3 player
4 Dan	most	has got after-school activities every week
5 Paula	fewest	plays video games every day
6 Mark	least amount of	watches TV every day
7 Francis	most	watches films every month
8 Laura	least amount of	has got free time every week

26 Work with a partner. Ask and answer questions about the sentences you made in 25.

Who's got the most books in her backpack?

Hannah has.

27 Choose the correct form of the words in brackets. With a partner, research the answer to each question.

1 Which country has got (the most / more) pet dogs: Germany or the UK?

2 Which animal spends (the least / less) time eating: a cat or a panda?

3 What is (larger / the largest) mammal on the planet: the elephant or the blue whale?

4 Which country gives the (least / fewest) homework: China, the UK or Finland?

5 Which animal is (slower / the slowest): a snail, a sloth or a turtle?

6 Which place is the (fewest / least) populated place on Earth: the Galapagos Islands, Easter Islands or Antarctica?

7 Which is (the biggest / bigger) planet in the solar system: Mars or Jupiter?

8 Which planet has got the (fewest / least) moons: Venus, Earth or Mars?

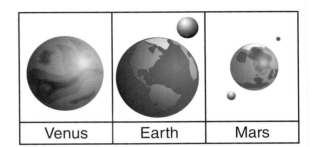

| Venus | Earth | Mars |

28 Complete the sentences with a word or phrase from the box.

| ancient | democracy | digest | herbivore |
| meat-eating | playwright | prime number | sloth |

1 Carnivores are 🐾 plants or animals.

2 Shakespeare was a famous English 🐾.

3 The Aztec and the Maya were 🐾 civilisations.

4 A 🐾 is a slow animal that sleeps upside down.

5 A 🐾 eats only plants and parts of plants.

6 A 🐾 can be divided only by 1 and itself.

7 When you 🐾 food, your body breaks it down.

8 A political system where the government is elected by the people is called a 🐾.

I Can

• **talk about school subjects and what I learn.**

• **identify some legacies of ancient civilisations.**

• **compare things using *more/most*, *fewer/ fewest*, *less/least*.**

How Well Do I Know It? Can I Use It?

1 Think about it. Read and draw. Practise.

😊 I know this.　　😐 I need more practice.　　🙁 I don't know this.

	PAGES			
Dreams: bring up a family, go on adventurous holidays, live in another country…	43	😊	😐	🙁
Super powers: read people's minds, become invisible…	55	😊	😐	🙁
School subjects: Music, English, Social Science…	66–67	😊	😐	🙁
Things we learn about: democracy, prime numbers…	66–67	😊	😐	🙁
What **will** you **be doing** ten years from now? I'll definitely **be studying** at a big university in the city. I probably **won't be living** in Europe. **Will** you **be running** a business? Yes, I **will.** / No, I **won't**.	46–47	😊	😐	🙁
If she **could have** one super power, she'**d fly.** If I **didn't have to go** to school, I'**d stay** at home all day. If you **could go** anywhere, where **would** you **go?** I'**d go** to Italy.	58–59	😊	😐	🙁
China's got **more** speakers of English **than** the USA. I've got **fewer** school subjects **than** my brother. Some teachers give **less** homework **than** others.	70–71	😊	😐	🙁
The Amazon rainforest has got **the most** species of plants and animals on Earth. Cheltenham is one of **the least** populated cities in the UK. Antarctica's got **the fewest** flowering plants of any continent.	70–71	😊	😐	🙁

2:42

2 Get ready.

A Number the lines of the dialogue in the correct order.
Then listen and check.

Calvin: Yeah, maybe. But I'd like to try it and see. How about you? If you could have just one kind of food every day, what would it be?

Calvin: Great! I love pizza! I wish I could eat pizza every day.

Calvin: What's for lunch tomorrow?

Calvin: Yuck. If I only ate salad, I'd feel hungry all the time. It's too boring.

Calvin: But I eat vegetables all the time… on pizza!

Hannah: No, you don't. If you ate pizza every day, you'd get sick of it.

Hannah: Let's see… Tomorrow's Friday. It looks like we'll be having pizza again.

Hannah: Well, it *wouldn't* be pizza. I think I'd have a salad every day.

Hannah: Salad isn't boring. You know, if I were you, I would try to eat more vegetables.

B Practise the dialogue in **A** with a partner.

C Ask and answer the questions with a partner.

1 How does Calvin feel about tomorrow's lunch? How about Hannah?
2 Does Calvin like vegetables? Explain.
3 If you could choose one food to eat every day, what would it be? Why?
4 What do you think would happen if you ate that food every day?

3 Get set.

✂ **STEP 1** Cut out the Mystery Classmate card on page 123 of your Activity Book.

▢ **STEP 2** Ask one classmate questions about him/her to fill in the card. Be sure to write neatly.

▢ **STEP 3** Mix up all the cards in a bag. Then each pupil takes one of the cards from the bag. Make sure it's not your own card. Now you're ready to **Go!**

4 Go!

A Work in a group. Take turns reading the information (except for the name) on your card aloud. Each group member copies the chart into a notebook and completes it by writing who he or she thinks the other group members are reading about.

Card number	Who read it?	Who do you think it's about?
Example	Andy	Anna
1	?	?
2	?	?
3	?	?
4	?	?

B Talk about your guesses. Give reasons for your choices.

> I think Andy's card is about Anna. She loves playing football and she'll be working in a hospital someday.

> I'm not sure. I don't think Anna likes chocolate.

C Each pupil says whose card he/she read in Step A. Check your guesses. Which person in your group solved the most mysteries?

5 Write about yourself in your notebook.

- If you could give any present to your best friend, what would it be? Why?
- What will you probably be doing twenty years from now?

All About Me Date:_____

_____

_____

How Well Do I Know It Now?

6 Look at page 78 and your notebook. Draw again.

A Use a different colour.

B Read and think.

I can start the next unit.

I can ask my teacher for help and then start the next unit.

I can practise and then start the next unit.

7 Rate this Checkpoint.

 very easy   easy   hard   very hard   fun   OK   not fun

MYSTERIES!

3:01

1 Can you identify these unsolved mysteries? Choose the name of the mystery from the box. Then listen carefully to check.

| Atlantis | Bermuda Triangle | crop circles | Kryptos | Nazca Lines |

1 A prosperous city can't just disappear, can it? Plato, the Greek philosopher, wrote a detailed description of this island paradise. Today, there's no sign of it. Some say it was swallowed up by the sea – the result of an earthquake or a flood. What do you think? Did the island city Plato wrote about ever exist?

Mystery: ⸮

2 Most drawings don't have to be looked at from 305 metres above. But that's the only way you can see these 1,000-year old geoglyphs in Peru. Scientists don't know who made these enormous drawings of animals, plants and humans or why. It makes you wonder, doesn't it?

Mystery: ⸮

3 Here in this region of the Atlantic Ocean, compasses won't help you with directions. Ships and planes simply disappear here. What's causing this to happen? Is it pirates, methane gas in the water, human error or something else? No one knows. It's puzzling… and a little scary.

Mystery: ⸮

2 Look at the photos. What's the mystery all about? Read and match the mysteries to the descriptions. Then listen to check.

1

Crop circles

2

The Bermuda Triangle

3

The Great Pyramids

4

Northern lights

a How were these constructed in ancient times without the benefit of modern tools? It doesn't seem possible.

b Modern scientists have come up with a solid theory to explain these brilliant colours and have got proof to support their theory.

c These perfect geometrical patterns seem to appear overnight. There's no scientific explanation for this phenomenon.

d No one can explain why things disappear in this area. It's an unsolved mystery.

3 Work with a partner. Talk about the mysteries.

They don't know the answer to the crop circles mystery, do they?

No, they don't. There's no scientific explanation.

THINK BIG Choose one of the mysteries in 2, do some research to find out more about it and come up with your own explanation.

3:04

Listen and read. Where did the dry lake bed get its name from?

A MYSTERY? NOT ANY MORE!

The Sailing Stones (Death Valley, California)

Imagine this: Rocks of different sizes, some weighing more than 300 kilos, sit on a dried-up flat lake bed that goes on for kilometres and kilometres. You would think that these rocks, especially the heaviest and biggest ones, would just sit in one spot forever, wouldn't you? Not the ones in Death Valley, California, in the USA! You can see them on the enormous expanse of dry lake bed called Racetrack Playa, which is named after these 'racing' stones. Much to everyone's surprise, many of them, including the really big and heavy ones, have actually moved hundreds of metres from their original locations – but, of course, this happened when no one was looking.

Not only did the rocks and stones move far, some seemed to have stopped and changed direction! A few even turned around and moved back to their original locations! Rocks moving on their own isn't possible, is it? As you read this, you're probably thinking of all kinds of weird explanations. Before blaming this on extraterrestrial beings, read on.

In the 1970s, some long-term studies of the phenomenon were carried out. Scientists now believe this: every year, the dry lake bed gets flooded with melted snow from the surrounding mountains. The water softens the soil in the old lake bed, turning it into slippery mud. Although no one has actually seen the rocks move, the best guess is that wind then moves the rocks across the slippery surface of the lake bed. Sounds like a logical explanation, doesn't it? Indeed it is, but without anyone actually witnessing the phenomenon, doubters remain.

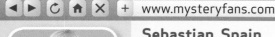

www.mysteryfans.com

Sebastian, Spain

Rocks that move? Pretty cool!

Emily, Australia

You don't really buy this whole story about stones moving, do you? Don't believe everything you read on the internet!

Liam, U.S.A.

Well, this story just happens to be true. I'm from California and the sailing stones have been studied since the 1940s. Even physicists have offered various theories. It's certainly not a hoax.

Georgina, UK

Wow, you're actually serious about these stones, aren't you? Do you guys believe that wind can actually make rocks move? Come on!

Detlef, Germany

I'm not totally convinced. There's got to be another explanation. Like pranksters, maybe?

Hiroto, Japan

I'm a geologist and rocks are my life. Believe me, Emily, these rocks really move! When the water level in the playa rises, the soil turns to mud and becomes slippery and strong winds cause the rocks to slide. Moderate winds can keep the rocks moving.

Liam, USA

Told you it's not a hoax. You're convinced now, aren't you?

READING COMPREHENSION

5 **Read and say** true **or** false.

1 People have seen the rocks move 100 metres.
2 No one doubts the explanation given by scientists.
3 Their theory involves wind and water.
4 The rocks don't all move in the same direction.
5 The heaviest rocks don't move at all.

THINK BIG Using objects or drawings, demonstrate and describe the various movements of the rocks in Racetrack Playa. Do you think pranksters are responsible for moving the rocks? Do you agree with scientists' explanation for the rocks moving? Why/Why not?

Language in Action

3:06

6 Listen and read. What's the big mystery?

James:	Hey, Kyle. Have you heard about Kryptos?
Kyle:	Ummm. I think so.
James:	You haven't got a clue, have you?
Kyle:	Yeah, I have. It's a video game, isn't it?
James:	Nope – not even close. It's a sculpture.
Kyle:	A sculpture of what?
James:	Let me see if I can find a picture... Yep, here's one.
Kyle:	Hmm, it's just letters of the alphabet. So why would anyone have a sculpture like that?
James:	The letters are really four encrypted messages. You need to work out the code to read the secret messages.
Kyle:	But nobody can read the messages, can they?
James:	Of course not! I think the idea is to challenge code breakers.
Kyle:	You're probably right. Has anyone decoded them yet?
James:	Yes, three have been decoded. But the fourth one is still a mystery.

7 Practise the dialogue in 6 with a partner.

3:07

8 Listen and match. Then choose the correct ending to the question.

1 Ancient people made these, (did they / didn't they)?

2 These are very beautiful, (are they / aren't they)?

3 People can't break the code, (can they / can't they)?

4 This place hasn't been found, (has it / hasn't it)?

a

b

c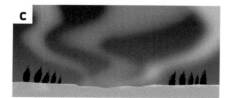

d

AFFIRMATIVE STATEMENTS	NEGATIVE TAGS	NEGATIVE STATEMENTS	POSITIVE TAGS
The geoglyphs **are** in Peru, Experts **have** explained them, We **solved** the mystery,	**aren't** they? **haven't** they? **didn't** we?	Atlantis **isn't** real, Scientists **haven't** found it, It **didn't** make sense,	**is** it? **have** they? **did** it?

Tip: Use question tags with falling intonation when you expect someone to agree with you.

9 Choose the correct question tags in brackets.

1 The northern lights are a natural phenomenon, (are they / aren't they)?

2 They are also called the aurora borealis, (are they / aren't they)?

3 The aurora borealis isn't a comet, (is it / isn't it)?

4 People in ancient times knew about the northern lights, (did they / didn't they)?

5 They're not visible in Asia, (are they / aren't they)?

6 Scientists haven't explained the aurora borealis yet, (have they / haven't they)?

10 Prepare to interview an archaeologist about Atlantis. Make question tags.

1. A: In your article, you claimed that Atlantis existed, 🔖
   B: Yes, I did...

2. A: You don't know the exact location of the city, 🔖
   B: No, I don't...

3. A: Your article claims that you have found artefacts, 🔖
   B: Yes, it does...

4. A: Most scientists disagree with your research, 🔖
   B: Yes, they do, but...

11 Write responses for the archaeologist in the interview in 10. Then role play the interview with a partner.

Listen and read. What is the aurora borealis?

AURORA BOREALIS
(THE NORTHERN LIGHTS)

Albert Einstein, whose work we still study today, once said this about nature: "What I see in nature is a magnificent structure that we can comprehend only very imperfectly and that must fill a thinking person with a feeling of humility." One could surely say this while looking at the aurora borealis!

For a long time, the aurora borealis was a mysterious natural phenomenon – no one clearly understood what caused it. Recently, science provided this explanation: the aurora borealis is caused by the interaction of solar winds with oxygen and nitrogen in the upper part of the atmosphere. These interactions excite the oxygen and nitrogen atoms, which changes their character. As the atoms return to their normal state, they give off colours. The different colours of an aurora mean that solar winds are interacting with different gases at different altitudes.

Such magical and mysterious beauty has inspired painters, poets and songwriters. But can art truly show the magnificence of this natural phenomenon? Look at these two pictures. Which one is a photo of a real aurora? Which one is a painting?

Read 12 again and say true or false.

1   The northern lights are the result of different elements interacting in Earth's atmosphere.

2   There is no explanation for the changing colours.

3   Albert Einstein explained what the aurora borealis was.

THINK BIG   Do you agree with Einstein that the beauty of nature should make a person feel humble? Why/Why not?

14 Listen and read. What is the yeti also known as?

Mysterious Findings

Stone Spheres (Costa Rica)

Take a look at the photograph. These perfectly round stone balls are no ordinary stones, are they? Obviously smoothed and shaped by someone or something, they vary in size, from the size of tennis balls to spheres that are eight feet in diameter and weigh 16 tons. In 1930, while clearing an area of the Costa Rican jungle, workers came upon a number of these balls, which are estimated to date back to 600 BC. Since then, several hundred have been discovered and they are all perfectly constructed! The mystery lies in working out who or what made them, what they were for and how they were made so perfectly.

The Abominable Snowman: The Yeti (Tibet)

You may have heard of the abominable snowman but like most people, you probably wonder if it's real or just a legend. The abominable snowman, also known as the *yeti,* is thought to be a creature resembling a gorilla. Many believe that the yeti lives in the Himalayan regions of Tibet and Nepal. Through the years, numerous expeditions have been organised to try to find evidence of the creature. So far, only footprints have been found with no proof that a yeti or any other creature made them. So why do people continue to believe the yeti exists? Because there's no proof that it doesn't.

15 Read 14 **again and say** stone spheres **or** yeti.

1 proof of existence
2 might be just a legend
3 discovered by accident
4 only footprints found
5 different sizes

16 Read this explanation for why the Sailing Stones move.

> ## What Causes the Sailing Stones to Move
>
> The Racetrack Playa in Death Valley gets seven to ten centimetres of rain a year but the rainfall comes in bursts. During the storms, the ground floods and the fine soil turns into mud and becomes very slippery. The winds, which can reach 145 kilometres per hour, can actually overcome the force of friction and cause the stones to move. Once the stones are already moving, much less powerful winds can keep them in motion.

17 Now copy and complete the missing words in the chart.

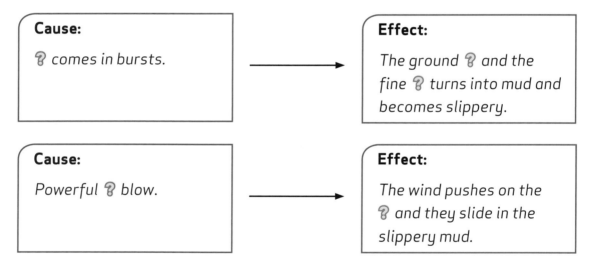

Cause:

❓ comes in bursts.

→

Effect:

The ground ❓ and the fine ❓ turns into mud and becomes slippery.

Cause:

Powerful ❓ blow.

→

Effect:

The wind pushes on the ❓ and they slide in the slippery mud.

18 In your notebook, write your own cause-and-effect paragraph. Choose a topic from your personal experience or from your Science or Social Science class. Before you write, make a chart like the one in 17. Use your chart to write the paragraph. Share your paragraph with the class.

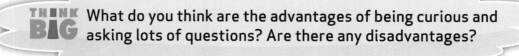

THINK BIG What do you think are the advantages of being curious and asking lots of questions? Are there any disadvantages?

19 Is curiosity important? Say which statements you agree with. Then discuss your opinions with a partner.

1 Curiosity makes us ask questions and questions help us learn.

2 Curiosity makes us unhappy and dissatisfied.

3 Curiosity leads to answers or solutions.

4 Curiosity encourages us to be creative.

5 Curiosity leads to inventions and discoveries.

6 Curiosity makes us look indecisive, like we don't know something.

20 Curious minds solve mysteries. How curious are you? Keep a curiosity diary for a week.

1 Copy these suggestions into your notebook:

Ask questions. / Be observant. / Find answers. / Study one new topic every day. / Try something new. / Read a lot!

2 Write in your diary every day. Give details that show your curiosity.

3 When your diary is complete, discuss it with a partner.

> *Monday, 17ᵗʰ March*
>
> *I was observant. I looked at a frog under a magnifying glass.*

PROJECT

At Ringing Rocks Park in Pennsylvania, USA, when you hit the rocks with a hammer, they sound like bells. That's unusual, isn't it? But it's true. And no one knows why it happens.

21 Did the things you read in this unit make you curious? Learn more about mysterious earth or science phenomena.

A Make a booklet with a partner. Research information about two mysteries. Use these headers for each topic:

- General Information
- Research Done
- Theories Found
- My Conclusion

B When you have finished, share your booklet with another pair.

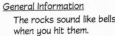

Mystery #1:
Ringing Rocks Park,
Pennsylvania, USA

General Information
The rocks sound like bells when you hit them.

Research Done
http://www.travelandleisure.com/travel-guide/bucks-county/activities/ringing-rocks-park

Theories Found
There are no explanations for this phenomenon.

My Conclusion
I think they must be made of something unusual.

Listening and Speaking

3:13

22 Listen, read and repeat.

1 un **2** inter **3** re **4** pre **5** super

3:14

23 Listen and blend the sounds.

1 un-h-a-pp-y unhappy   **2** inter-n-a-t-io-n-a-l international

3 re-c-y-c-le recycle   **4** pre-u-s-ed preused

5 Super-m-a-n Superman   **6** re-d-u-ce reduce

3:15

24 Listen and chant.

Celebrate International Earth Day!
Recycle your Superman T-shirt
And your pre-washed bottles.
Reduce unhealthy food,
Try healthy food! It's good!

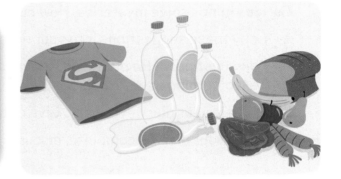

25 Work in a small group. Do a survey. Which mystery is your favourite? Make a graph to show what your classmates' favourite mystery is.

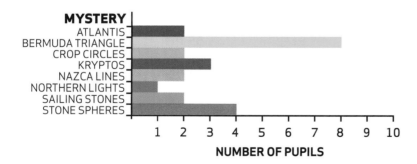

MYSTERY

ATLANTIS
BERMUDA TRIANGLE
CROP CIRCLES
KRYPTOS
NAZCA LINES
NORTHERN LIGHTS
SAILING STONES
STONE SPHERES

1 2 3 4 5 6 7 8 9 10
NUMBER OF PUPILS

26 Ask and answer questions about the results. Use question tags when you can.

The Bermuda Triangle is our favourite mystery, isn't it?

I think it's because it's still unsolved.

Yeah. I wonder why.

Maybe but I think it's because it's creepy.

27 Complete the sentences using question tags. Then give answers to show you agree or disagree.

> I think so. We can't solve them unless we investigate them.

1 All unsolved mysteries are worth investigating, ❓

2 Most unsolved mysteries are hoaxes, ❓

3 Some mysteries can't be solved even with scientific research, ❓

4 Having a curious mind is important, ❓

5 Curiosity makes new discoveries and inventions possible, ❓

6 Einstein had a curious mind, ❓

7 The Bermuda Triangle mystery hasn't been explained, ❓

8 You haven't heard of the Ringing Rocks, ❓

9 Scientists know what causes the northern lights phenomenon, ❓

10 You know about the yeti, ❓

28 Complete the sentences with words from the box.

| phenomenon | proof | scientific | theory | unsolved |

1 So far, there is no ❓ explanation for how the stones became so perfectly round.

2 One ❓ that explains the mystery of Atlantis is that it disappeared during a large earthquake.

3 Actually, there's no reliable ❓ that the city of Atlantis ever existed.

4 The aurora borealis is a natural ❓ that has been explained.

5 The mystery of the stone spheres is still ❓.

I Can

- discuss mysterious phenomena.

- confirm information using question tags.

WHY IS IT FAMOUS?

3:16

1 Work with a partner. Look at the map and the pictures of the places. Match the places to the names in the box. Then listen to check.

1
?

2
?

3
?

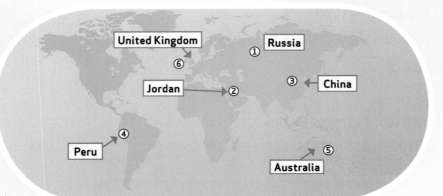

United Kingdom

⑥

① Russia

Jordan ②

③ ← China

Peru ④

⑤

Australia

City of Petra
Forbidden City
Machu Picchu
St. Basil's Cathedral
Stonehenge
Sydney Opera House

4
?

5
?

6
?

2 Share your results with the class. Who identified the most places correctly?

3 Discuss in small groups.
- Have you ever heard about any of these places? Which ones?
- Why are they famous?

4 Look at the photos and read the information about each. Then listen and complete.

**1 Big Ben
(the Elizabeth Tower)**

Location:
  London, UK
When it was completed: ?

2 Taj Mahal

Location:
  Agra, ?
When it was built:
  between 1632–1654

3 Temple of Borobudur

Location:
  Central Java, Indonesia
When it was built:
  in the ? and ? centuries

4 Great Sphinx of Giza

Location:
  Giza, ?
When it was built:
  probably between
  2558–2532 BC

5 Statue of Liberty

Location:
  New York City Harbour, USA
When it was dedicated: ?

**6 Pyramid of Kukulcán
(El Castillo) at
Chichén Itzá**

Location:
  Yucatan Peninsula, Mexico
When it was built:
  around ? AD

5 Look at 4. Listen and match the descriptions to the places. Note down any new information you learn.

6 Work with a partner. Talk about the famous places and things. Give as much information as you can.

Is Big Ben a clock, a tower or a bell?

It's a bell. It hangs inside the Elizabeth Tower in London.

 THINK BIG Choose a famous landmark in your country, research the facts you don't know about it and present it to the class.

3:20

7 Listen and read. What is another name for Easter Island?

The Mysteries of Easter Island

For hundreds of years, Easter Island has been a place shrouded in mystery. Have the mysteries of this faraway island finally been solved?

Full of mysteries, Easter Island is a small island that sits in the Pacific Ocean, about 3,500 kilometres to the west of Chile, South America. It is a volcanic island that may once have had a population of 7,000–17,000 people. Today, there are only 4,000 people who live on the island.

Easter Island, known as Rapa Nui to the original settlers, was discovered by Dutch explorers on Easter Day in 1722. Most people know Easter Island today because of the giant statues there, called *moai*.

For a long time, no one was sure about where the people of Rapa Nui were from. Thanks to DNA testing of old bones, we now know that the original people of Rapa Nui were from Polynesia.

> **For many years, the statues were also the subject of mystery.**

For many years, the statues were also the subject of mystery. The faces of the statues looked expressionless. Many scientists thought the statues represented dead ancestors. In 1979, scientist Sergio Rapu Haoa discovered that long ago the statues had eyes that were made of coral. Since his discovery, many of the eyes of the moai have been restored. With eyes, the statues' faces look very different. They look like proud, strong leaders who watch over Rapa Nui.

Probably the biggest mystery about the statues today is still

Moai on Easter Island

this: how were these statues – most of which are over 4 metres tall and weigh more than 12 tons – moved from the quarry where they were carved out of volcanic rock to various locations around the island?

Some scientists believe the Rapa Nui people used trees to move the statues. They think the tree trunks were used as rollers, or sleds, to pull the statues across the island. Other scientists, however, believe the statues were 'walked' across the island. They think ropes were used to rock the statues from side to side, moving them forward a little each time they were rocked. And some people even believe that the statues were moved by aliens with sophisticated technology who helped the Rapa Nui people put the statues in new locations.

Scientists have discovered a lot about this ancient culture over just the last fifty years. Maybe someday they will solve all of its mysteries.

Moai with eyes restored

READING COMPREHENSION

8 Read and say true or false. Compare your answers with a partner.

1 The population of Easter Island today is about 7,000.

2 Easter Island is famous because it was discovered on Easter Day.

3 DNA of old bones was used to find out where the people of Rapa Nui were from.

4 In 1979, a scientist discovered that the moai once had eyes that were made of coral.

5 One unsolved mystery is how the statues were moved to different locations on the island.

 How do you think the moai were moved to their locations around the island? Explain.
What other places do you know of that hold mysteries like this?

Language in Action

9 Listen and read. What places can Juan and his family visit without going very far?

Juan: Do you know what Mum told me? We don't appreciate things that are close to us – right here in Taos.

Dad: She's right. This town's got a lot of history.

Juan: Remember the family who was visiting from London last summer?

Dad: I do. They were really excited about seeing the old churches here.

Juan: Yeah, and we had never been to *any* that were on their list! They were really surprised, weren't they?

Dad: Yeah. But thanks to that family, we finally got to see the inside of the Church of San Francisco de Asís.

Juan: The one that was rebuilt? That was cool. You know, Dad, maybe we should visit more of the famous places that are around us. How about the Taos Ski Valley? It's known all over the world!

Dad: I *knew* you had a reason for bringing this up. You want to go on a ski trip!

10 Practise the dialogue in 9 with a partner.

11 Listen and match. Then complete the sentences with the correct form of a verb from the box.

> build   bury
> design   take

a

b

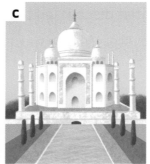
c

d

1 It ❓ on an island.

2 The photographs ❓ in Mexico.

3 The emperor's wife ❓ in this place.

4 It ❓ by an architect from Denmark.

Active	Passive
Archaeologists discovered Machu Picchu in 1911.	Machu Picchu **was discovered** in 1911 (by archaeologists).

12 Say whether each sentence is active or passive.

1 The Taj Mahal is visited by millions of tourists each year.

2 Alexandre Gustave Eiffel designed Paris's Eiffel Tower.

3 Two hundred thousand workers constructed the Forbidden City.

4 Petra, Jordan, was made a new wonder of the world by millions of voters.

5 The Sydney Opera House was opened to the public in 1973.

> Leonardo da Vinci is the famous artist and inventor **who painted** the Mona Lisa. The Eiffel Tower is a landmark **that has become** the symbol of Paris, France.
>
> **Tip:** A relative clause describes a noun. The relative pronouns *who* and *that* are used to describe people; *that* is used to describe things.

13 Rewrite the two sentences as one sentence in your notebook.

1 The Statue of Liberty is a landmark. It has become a symbol of welcome.

2 Van Gogh was a famous Dutch painter. He painted *Starry Night*.

3 The Leaning Tower of Pisa is a famous landmark. It leans to one side.

4 The Taj Mahal is a beautiful mausoleum. It was built in memory of Mumtaz Mahal.

5 Michelangelo was a famous artist. He painted the ceiling of the Sistine Chapel.

6 King Tutankhamen was a young king. He ruled Egypt during the 18th dynasty.

7 The Burj Al Arab is a luxurious hotel. It's located in Dubai.

8 Santiago Calatrava is a Spanish architect. He designed the Turning Torso, the tallest building in Sweden.

9 The Alhambra is a palace in Andalusia, Spain. It was originally constructed as a fortress.

10 The Great Wall of China is a type of fortification. It is 21,196 kilometres long.

3:26

14 Listen and read. Who discovered the ancient pyramids in Mexico City?

CONTENT WORDS

archaeologist   artefact   carved   pharaoh   site   tomb

ACCIDENTAL DISCOVERIES

Accidental discoveries, like the ones described on this page, are sometimes the most important discoveries ever made!

Ancient Pyramids in Mexico City

In 1978, a new subway system for Mexico City was being constructed. As the workers were digging, they discovered a huge carved stone! The stone was over three metres around and about 30 centimetres thick. It weighed a little over 8.5 tons. Archaeologists were brought in. In addition to the carved stone, they discovered a pyramid! Soon scientists found six other pyramids that had been added to or built on top of the original one. Scientists dated the original pyramid to the year 1325 AD. Over 7,000 different artefacts were found at the site. If you visit the Zócalo, which is the main plaza in the heart of the city, you can see the artefacts in a museum.

King Tutankhamen's Tomb

The discovery of King Tutankhamen's tomb in the Valley of the Kings in Egypt might be the most famous accidental discovery of its kind. The Valley is home to more than 60 tombs in which ancient pharaohs and kings are buried. King Tutankhamen's tomb is the most well-preserved ancient tomb that has ever been found. The tomb survived 3,000 years, even though robbers and floods destroyed many of the other tombs from that region. The artefacts from the tomb that once belonged to King Tutankhamen can now be seen in the Cairo Museum in Egypt.

15 Read 14 **again and say** Mexico City **or** Egypt.

1   3,000 years old

2   almost 700 years old

3   not in a city plaza

4   six other similar constructions in the area

3:28

16 Listen and read. Which is the oldest of the seven new world wonders?

THE NEW 7 WORLD WONDERS

How about a bicycle trip to the New Seven Wonders of the World?

Your route is already mapped out. So grab your bike and get ready to ride!

1 *PETRA: Possibly built as early as the 6ᵗʰ century BC* — The capital of an ancient empire, this city's structures were carved into rock and sandstone.

2 *TAJ MAHAL: Built between 1632–1654* — When Mumtaz Mahal, the wife of Emperor Shah Jahan, died in childbirth, the grieving emperor built the mausoleum in her memory.

3 *GREAT WALL OF CHINA: Built from the 5ᵗʰ century BC to the 16ᵗʰ century AD* — This wall was built more than 2,000 years ago to keep enemies out.

4 *KUKULCÁN PYRAMID AT CHICHÉN ITZÁ: Built sometime between the 11ᵗʰ and the 13ᵗʰ centuries AD* — Chichén Itzá is an archaeological site on the Yucatan Peninsula. Kukulcán, a 30-metre-high pyramid and temple, is its most famous landmark.

5 *MACHU PICCHU: Built in the early 15ᵗʰ century AD* — This ancient Incan city is located 2,430 metres above sea level and consists of 150 buildings. Its most famous structure, the Temple of the Sun, is made of solid rock.

6 *CHRIST THE REDEEMER STATUE: Built between 1922–1931* — Standing 38 metres tall at the top of a mountain is a statue of Christ with his arms outstretched. The statue looks out over the city of Rio de Janeiro, Brazil.

7 *ROMAN COLOSSEUM: Built between 72–80 AD* — During the Roman Empire, the Colosseum was used for battles between gladiators and for other forms of entertainment.

17 Which of the new seven world wonders was built:

a to show great love?

b for religious reasons?

c for protection from enemies?

d for competition and entertainment?

THINK BIG Work with a partner. Design a structure that you would want people to discover in the future. Discuss these questions as you work on your concept.

• Where will you build your structure? What materials will you use?

• What will be its unique features that might make it famous someday?

Present your design to the class. Vote on the best one.

18 Read the report. Then copy the idea web and use the information to complete it.

Australia is one of the seven continents but it's also a country. It's known as the smallest continent in the world. Do you know why it's called 'the land down under'? It's because Australia is located below the equator.

More than 22 million people live in Australia. Aborigines are the original inhabitants of Australia but people from many different countries have come to Australia to live. Today, most people in Australia speak English.

The capital of Australia is Canberra. Other big and important cities in Australia are Sydney, Melbourne, Brisbane and Perth.

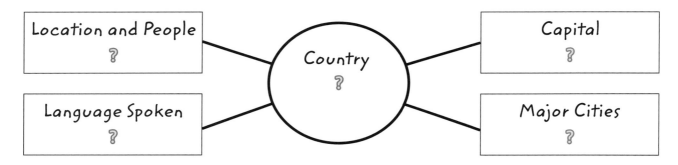

Location and People		
Language Spoken	Country	Capital
	?	Major Cities

19 Choose a country to write a report about. Do research to find out facts about the country. Write them in an idea web.

20 Use your idea web to write your report. Share it with the class.

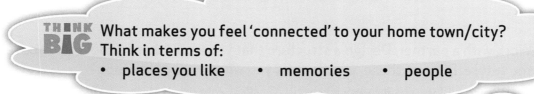

THINK BIG What makes you feel 'connected' to your home town/city?
Think in terms of:
- places you like
- memories
- people

21 Look at this list of features. Has your town or city (or a nearby town or city) got any of these? Copy the list and write the names and locations. Add any additional attractions to your list.

- a statue of a famous person or historical event
- an art museum
- a history, anthropological or science museum
- a concert hall or event centre
- a stadium or athletic field
- old houses or other historical structures
- religious places that are historically or culturally important
- a beautiful park or garden
- a famous restaurant
- a college or university

PROJECT

> The Clock Tower in Chetbury was built in 1870. It used to be a village hall and a fire station. Today, it's a historic building with shops in it.

22 Work in a small group. Prepare a map for a bicycle trip to six famous or interesting places in your town/city, county or country.

1 See page 101 for ideas.

2 Make a map.

3 Prepare a brief oral presentation of your map. Make notes on index cards. List information like this about each place:
  - the location
  - a short description of the place
  - when the place was built
  - why it was built

4 Tell your classmates about each place as you share your map with them.

Listening and Speaking

3:29

23 Listen, read and repeat.

1 able **2** ful **3** ly

3:30

24 Listen and blend the sounds.

1 c-o-m-f-or-t-able comfortable **2** p-ea-ce-ful peaceful

3 d-ee-p-ly deeply **4** w-a-sh-able washable

5 b-eau-t-i-ful beautiful **6** s-l-ow-ly slowly

3:31

25 Listen and chant.

> I feel so comfortable
> On my soft pillow.
> I breathe deeply.
> I breathe slowly
> And I have a peaceful sleep.

26 Work in a small group. Play a guessing game.

A Use the words and phrases from the boxes to create a list of clues for a guessing game.

> cathedral city island mausoleum monument place statue temple tower

> is a/an

> is famous for / located in

B Take turns giving clues to your group. Keep giving information until someone in your group guesses correctly.

This is an island that's famous for giant rocks.

No, not Stonehenge. Stonehenge isn't an island. The giant rocks are statues.

Correct!

I'm not sure. Stonehenge?

I know! It's Easter Island.

27 Complete each sentence with a word from the box.

mausoleum	monument	pyramids	Statue	temple	tower

1 The ❓ are burial places for ancient Egyptian pharaohs.

2 Borobudur in Indonesia is a famous Buddhist ❓ dedicated to Buddha.

3 The ❓ of Liberty was given to the United States by the people of France.

4 The Taj Mahal is actually a ❓ where Mumtaz Mahal is buried.

5 Big Ben is a bell that's located in London's most famous clock ❓.

6 Stonehenge is a famous ❓ whose original purpose remains a mystery.

28 Combine the pairs of sentences into one. Use who or that.

1 Machu Picchu is an ancient city. It is 2,430 metres above sea level in the Andes Mountains. ❓

2 The *moai* are giant rock statues. They were found on Easter Island. ❓

3 Christ the Redeemer is a famous statue. It stands over the city of Rio de Janeiro. ❓

4 Michelangelo was an Italian Renaissance artist. He created the statue known as *David*. ❓

5 The Great Sphinx is a monument. It has remained a mystery to this day. ❓

6 Johan Vermeer was a Dutch painter. He painted *Girl with a Pearl Earring* in 1665. ❓

7 The Parthenon is a beautiful temple. It's located on the Acropolis in Athens. ❓

8 Marie Curie was a Polish chemist. She's famous for her research in radioactivity. ❓

I Can

- talk about famous places and structures around the world.
- describe places and structures using the passive voice and relative clauses.

unit 9 THAT'S ENTERTAINMENT!

4:01

1 Read about some performers, films and books from the world of entertainment. Guess the name of each one. Then listen carefully to check.

1 The first three films in this series made almost 1.5 billion euros at the box office and more than 330 million euros in DVD sales. The fourth film in this series was sold out in cinemas before it was even released.

2 This young singer-songwriter has won many awards, including Artist of the Year and Best New Artist. This musician has got more than 25 million followers on Twitter and has sold more than 15 million albums.

3 This book series has sold 450 million copies, making it the best-selling book series in history. It has now been translated into sixty-seven languages. The last four books in this series have set records as the fastest-selling books ever.

4 This singer's second album alone has earned her seven Grammy Awards, two Brit Awards, three American Music Awards and at least fourteen other awards. This person has sold more than 26 million albums and has written and sung an original song for *Skyfall*, the twenty-third James Bond film.

5 This actor was recently named the highest-paid teenage actor in Hollywood. He has appeared in many TV shows and films but is best known for his role as Jacob Black.

2 Listen. Copy the diary into your notebook and complete it with the things that Becky has planned to do. Use names of events from the box. Then match the events to the pictures below.

> book signing   comic book exhibition   concert   festival   film premiere

January ❓ ❀   March ❓

                April ❓

February ❓   May ❓

❓

❓

❓

❓

❓

3 Work with a partner. Talk about Becky's activities for next year and what she said she was going to do each month.

What did Becky say she was doing in January?

She said she was going to an Adele concert.

THINK BIG What do you consider good entertainment. Why?

4 Listen and read. Which reviewer hopes Stanley's third album will be better than his second?

www.reviewsbykids.com

▶ TV Shows

▶ Films

▶ Books

▶ Clothes

▼ Music
- mp3
- Best Sellers
- Today's Deals
- CDs

CUSTOMER REVIEWS
You Know It!

Stanley Scott
YOU KNOW IT!

5 stars: ★ ★ ★ ★ ★ 139 reviews
4 stars: ★ ★ ★ ★ ☆ 82 reviews
3 stars: ★ ★ ★ ☆ ☆ 17 reviews
2 stars: ★ ★ ☆ ☆ ☆ 2 reviews
1 star: ★ ☆ ☆ ☆ ☆ 7 reviews

Display reviews by most helpful:

★ ★ ★ ★ ★ **Love it! Love it! Love it!**
by Little_Kitty
I really liked Stanley's first album but I didn't know what to expect with the second one. My best friend said this album was even better than the first one and he was so right! There's a rumour that it's going to be nominated for the Best Album Award. How cool is that!

★ ★ ★ ★ ★ **This was so worth the wait!**
by music_lover_2003
I am a huge Stanley fan. I have been waiting for this album for SO LONG and it's finally HERE! My friends and I bought it as soon as it came out. I'm going to a concert of his next week. I can't wait!

★ ★ ★ ★ ☆ **Not as good as the first one but still really good.**
by JJ_keyboards
Scott's first album was pretty good. Everybody could see that this guy had a lot of talent but then the recording companies started to control Scott and his music. The sound in the new album isn't as good as it was in the first. I still like Scott's music a lot so I bought the new album. But I'm hoping that he'll go back to his old sound when he makes his third album!

★ ★ ☆ ☆ ☆ **Not bad but a little disappointing.**
by star_fan

I bought Stanley Scott's first album and I really liked it. My friend told me that Stanley had been working with my favourite singer, Sasha Littleton, so I thought maybe the music in this album would be different from the first one. Well, it's OK but I was a little disappointed. I'm still going to see him at Fairlop festival next month and hope he'll play most of his old songs.

★ ☆ ☆ ☆ ☆ **AWFUL!**
by music_for_life

I think this kid has got some talent but this is NOT music! It's the product of a big recording company. It's their sound, not Stanley Scott's. The lyrics, the music, everything is so boring. I'm not going to buy his next one if it's like this. There's no creativity in this album at all! Even kids like me know the difference between real music and stuff like this.

READING COMPREHENSION

5 Match the two parts to create a summary of each of the five reviews.

1   Little_Kitty said…
2   Music_lover_2003 said…
3   JJ_keyboards said that…
4   Star_fan said…
5   Music_for_life said that…

a   there was no creativity in Stanley's second album.

b   Stanley's album was going to be nominated for an award.

c   Stanley's second album wasn't as good as his first.

d   he was going to see Stanley at a festival next month.

e   she was going to see Stanley perform next week.

 THINK BIG What did most people who reviewed Stanley's second album think of it? Where do you usually see music and film reviews? Why do people write reviews? Why do you think people read them?

Language in Action

4:05

6 Listen and read. What did Darren's mum say?

Carol: What are you doing?

Darren: I'm counting the money that I've saved up from my pocket money.

Carol: Here, let me help. So what are you going to spend this on?

Darren: I want to go to the comic book exhibition. Hannah's dad is taking her and Mum said that I could go with them. But I've got to buy the ticket myself.

Carol: Why do you want to spend all your money on that?

Darren: Because I love comic books! And I've never been to a comic book exhibition before.

Carol: Laura said she was going, too, so there will be three of you there.

Darren: Great! It's going to be brilliant. There's an art competition and I'm entering my comic book.

Carol: Good idea. You're great at drawing.

7 Practise the dialogue in 6 with a partner.

4:06

8 Listen and match. Then complete the sentences using the correct words from the box.

| fantastic | good |
| impressive | stunning |

1 A reviewer said the animation was ❓.

2 Luke said it was really ❓.

3 A boy said it was ❓.

4 Her friend said it was ❓.

a

b

c

d

Direct speech	Reported speech
Claire said, "The album **isn't** as good as the last one."	Claire said (that) the album **wasn't** as good as the last one.
Josh said, "I**'m going** to the premiere."	Josh said (that) he **was going** to the premiere.
Tip: Change the verb in the reported statement from the present simple to the past simple or from the present continuous to the past continuous.	

9 Read what each person is saying. Rewrite their words in your notebook as reported speech.

1   Adele is my favourite singer.

Alana

2   I like One Direction better than Adele.

Mike

3   My parents are going to the opera.

Shari

10 Change the direct speech to reported speech.

1   My mum said, "His concerts are expensive."

2   Julia said, "The new vampire film is getting bad reviews."

3   Rosie said, "I'm going to win the competition."

4   Alex said, "There are only a few tickets left."

5   James said, "I'm reading a great book at the moment."

6   Harry said, "The concert starts at 8."

7   Emma said, "Dad's coming to pick me up after the festival".

8   George said, "Her new album is much better than her last one".

11 Listen and read. When did Tetris become popular?

CONTENT WORDS

arcade   coins   compete   graphics   national   scores   shortage

THE HISTORY OF VIDEO GAMES

Video games are so popular – they're even used in classrooms. Let's take a look at how it all started...

1952–1972

There were a number of different games created in the United States during this period, including *Tennis for Two, Spacewar!* and *Chase*.

1980

Used by the government for training purposes, the first-ever 3-D video game, called *Battlezone,* was created in the United States.

1989

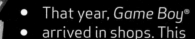

That year, *Game Boy*® arrived in shops. This black-and-white Japanese video game player became popular with the puzzle game *Tetris*.

2004

Wii™ was invented. It was a big hit because people could play a video game with their whole body, not just with their fingers.

1972

Invented in the United States, *Pong*® was too big and expensive for people's homes at first. Many people wanted to play *Pong* in their living rooms. Three years later, they got their wish!

1978

Space Invaders® was the first-ever arcade game to track and display high scores. Its popularity in Japan caused a national shortage of coins! Later, game developers created multiplayer games, which enabled people to compete at home.

Future

With so much change over the last fifty years, what's next?

12 Read 11 again and say the year.

1 People could play *Pong*® in their living rooms.

2 People could buy *Game Boy*® in shops.

3 A group of people could play a game together and compete.

4:11

13 Listen and read. Which instrument was played by one of the Beatles?

Unique Musical Instruments

Around the world, there are many instruments that are unique to a specific culture or area. This article takes a look at just a few.

BAGPIPES

A bagpipe consists of a bag, pipes, drones and a chanter (keyboard). This instrument is particularly popular on Burns Night, 25th January, when Scottish people celebrate the birthday of the Scottish poet, Robert Burns.

SITAR

The sitar is a stringed instrument used in classical Indian music. It's common in India, Pakistan and Bangladesh. It's not a guitar but looks similar. George Harrison played one and some of the Beatles' songs featured this instrument.

STEEL DRUMS

In the 1700s, these drums were created out of oil drums to celebrate Carnival in Trinidad and Tobago. This instrument contains a number of different notes as the steel has been bent to create these sounds. Many musicians play six to eight drums at a time.

ALPINE HORN

This pastoral instrument is associated with herdsmen, especially those in mountainous regions. Historians believe it was used as many as 2,000 years ago by Celtic tribes. Most alpine horns (or alphorns) are carved out of spruce wood and they've got a mellow, echoey sound.

14 Read 13 again and say the instrument.

1 You can play six of them at the same time.

2 It's an ancient instrument that was used by the Celts.

3 It's very popular in Scotland.

THINK BIG What unique instruments are used in your country? What's special about the instruments?

Writing | Film review

15 Read the film review. What does the reviewer say about the story, the acting and the special effects? Discuss with a partner.

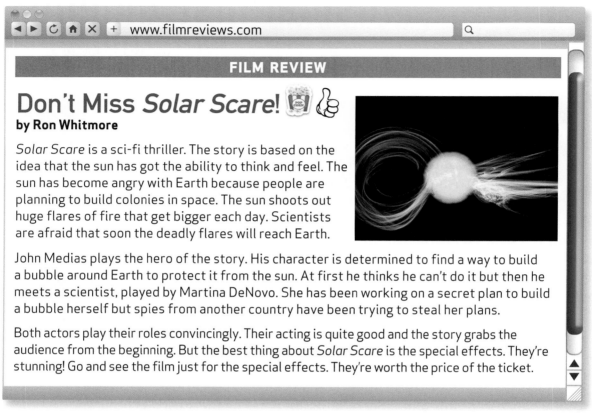

www.filmreviews.com

FILM REVIEW

Don't Miss *Solar Scare*! 🍿👍
by Ron Whitmore

Solar Scare is a sci-fi thriller. The story is based on the idea that the sun has got the ability to think and feel. The sun has become angry with Earth because people are planning to build colonies in space. The sun shoots out huge flares of fire that get bigger each day. Scientists are afraid that soon the deadly flares will reach Earth.

John Medias plays the hero of the story. His character is determined to find a way to build a bubble around Earth to protect it from the sun. At first he thinks he can't do it but then he meets a scientist, played by Martina DeNovo. She has been working on a secret plan to build a bubble herself but spies from another country have been trying to steal her plans.

Both actors play their roles convincingly. Their acting is quite good and the story grabs the audience from the beginning. But the best thing about *Solar Scare* is the special effects. They're stunning! Go and see the film just for the special effects. They're worth the price of the ticket.

He said that the best thing was the special effects!

Cool! I'll check it out this weekend.

16 Follow these steps to write your own film review. It can be positive or negative.

1 Choose a film you have seen recently. Describe what type of film it is.

2 Briefly describe the story.

3 What did you think about the story, the acting and other features?

4 Write notes.

5 Use your notes to write your review.

> **TIP**
> Try to use vivid adjectives as you write, for example: *stunning, captivating, tense, gripping,* etc.

17 Read a classmate's review. Report back to the class to share what your classmate said about the film.

18 Read the four different opinions. Match each opinion to an item in the box.

> **a** an exhibition
> **b** a concert (2x)
> **c** a video game

1 It was the best live musical performance I've ever seen.

2 The event, which was held in a dark hall, was badly organised and too busy for me!

3 It was the most exciting game I've ever played. I can't wait until they launch the sequel.

4 The music was much too loud. I won't be going to one again anytime soon.

PROJECT

19 Make an Opinion Map. **Work in a small group.**

1 Choose a film, book, comic book or album that everyone in your group knows.

2 Share your opinions about it.

3 Record what each person thinks about it on an Opinion Map.

4 Present your Opinion Map to the class:

We reviewed Lady Gaga's new album. Ali said it wasn't as good as her last one, etc.

Ali: It's not as good as her last one.

Kyle: It's great to listen to while I'm doing my homework!

Lady Gaga's New Album

Lisa: The music is too loud! It drowns out her voice.

Sam: The best! It's better than any of her other albums.

TIP

Show interest when people share their opinions. Here are some expressions:
I think so, too.   Why do you say that?
That's interesting.   Really? I don't agree.

 THINK BIG Why is it important to listen to different opinions? Think in terms of:
• respect   • having an open mind   • learning something new

Listening and Speaking

4:12

20 Listen, read and repeat.

1 sion   **2** tion   **3** ation

4:13

21 Listen and blend the sounds.

1 t-e-l-e-v-i-sion   television   **2** f-i-c-tion   fiction

3 c-e-l-e-b-r-ation   celebration   **4** d-e-c-i-sion   decision

5 o-p-tion   option   **6** i-n-v-i-t-ation   invitation

4:14

22 Listen and chant.

> I've got an invitation
> To a birthday celebration.
> We'll watch science fiction
> Films on television.
> Now that's a good decision!

23 Work with a partner. Copy and complete this chart for yourself. Then write your partner's answers.

What's your favourite... ?	Me	My partner
animated film		
action film		
comedy film		
comic book		
video game		
actor		
singer		
song		
album		

24 With your partner, talk about three of the items on the list. Why are those your favourites?

> *Krypton Kid* is my favourite animated film. The animation is brilliant. The ending is amazing!

116 Unit 9

25 Complete each sentence with a word from the box.

| book signing | comic book exhibition | concert | festival | premiere | review |

1 I wanted to go to the Ne-Yo last night but it was sold out. I read Gayle Smart's of it and she said it was amazing.

2 Did you hear? The Stamford Summer Brit-pop Music has been announced for June next year. I can't wait!

3 Do you like comic books? Have you ever been to a ? If you enjoy reading comic books, this event will blow your mind.

4 Did you hear? *Flipped* is now a film! The is next week. And the author will be at a event at Bookspace on the same day.

26 Read the dialogue. Then answer the questions using reported speech.

Brian: What are you doing this weekend?

Carol: I'm going to a hip-hop festival. It starts tomorrow.

Brian: Cool. You're pretty good at dancing, aren't you?

Carol: I *love* dancing! I'm going to be in a competition next week.

Brian: Wow! So, who's going to be at the festival?

Carol: Jessie J, Kelly Rowland, Diddy and plenty more.

Brian: It sounds amazing!

Carol: Yeah. Want to come?

Brian: Sorry, I can't. I'm babysitting all day tomorrow.

1 What did Carol say she was doing this weekend?

2 What did Carol say she was going to do next week?

3 What did Brian say about the festival when he heard who was going to be there?

4 What did Brian say he was doing instead of going to the festival?

I Can

- **talk about entertainment.**

- **talk about people's opinions.**

- **report what people say.**

How Well Do I Know It? Can I Use It?

1 Think about it. Read and draw. Practise.

☺ I know this.   😐 I need more practice.   ☹ I don't know this.

	PAGES			
Mysteries: Atlantis, Bermuda Triangle, crop circles…	82-83	☺	😐	☹
Mystery-related words: phenomenon, unsolved, proof…	82-83	☺	😐	☹
Structures: palace, statue, tower…	94-95	☺	😐	☹
Famous places: Statue of Liberty, Taj Mahal…	94-95	☺	😐	☹
Entertainment: concert, film premiere, book signing…	107	☺	😐	☹
The Sailing Stones **are** in California, **aren't** they? The agent **can** break this code, **can't** he? She**'s got** a curious mind, **hasn't** she? The aurora borealis **isn't** a real mystery, **is** it? We **can't** see crop circles from the ground, **can** we? They **haven't** got all the answers, **have** they?	86-87	☺	😐	☹
The Taj Mahal **is visited** by millions of tourists each year. Machu Picchu **was discovered** in 1911 (by archaeologists).	98-99	☺	😐	☹
Leonardo da Vinci was the famous artist and inventor **who** painted the *Mona Lisa*. The Eiffel Tower is a landmark **that** has become the symbol of Paris, France.	98-99	☺	😐	☹
Claire said, "The album **isn't** as good as the last one." She said the album **wasn't** as good as the last one. Dana said, "Paul**'s going** to a concert. She said that Paul **was going** to a concert.	110-111	☺	😐	☹

4:15

2 **Get ready.**

A Choose the correct word or phrase to complete the dialogue. Then listen and check.

Tina:	Hey, do you want to watch *Mystery Tour*?
Kevin:	I don't know. What's it about?
Tina:	It's a new show about scientists (who / who's) travel around the world and study mysterious places, like the Bermuda Triangle.
Kevin:	Oh, I've heard about that show! My friend at school said it (was / were) really good.
Tina:	Oops, wait a minute, Kevin. It's not on until 9:00. Your mum said your bedtime was at 8:30, (did / didn't) she?
Kevin:	That's during the week. On Saturdays I'm allowed to stay up until 9:30.
Tina:	Oh, lucky you. You can watch it, then.
Kevin:	So *Mystery Tour* is scary, right?
Tina:	Umm, not really. I think it's (make / made) for people (who's / that) like science. You're good at science, (are / aren't) you?
Kevin:	Yes, I am. But actually I like scary shows better, like *Dark Corners*.
Tina:	*Dark Corners*! That's a spooky show!
Kevin:	What's wrong with spooky? Anyway, it's not on any more. It (is dropped / was dropped) last month.
Tina:	Probably because it was too spooky.

B Practise the dialogue in **A** with a partner.

C Ask and answer the questions with a partner.

1 What is the TV show *Mystery Tour* about?

2 What has Kevin heard about the show?

3 Will Kevin be able to watch the show with Tina? Why/Why not?

4 Does the show sound interesting to you? Why/Why not?

Get set.

 STEP 1 Cut out the cards on page 125 of your Activity Book.

 STEP 2 Assign a group leader. The group leader gets a set of yellow cards, the group gets a set of green cards and each group member gets a set of orange cards. Now you're ready to **Go!**

 Go!

A   Work in a group of five.

- The group leader takes the yellow card. Each other member takes one of the green cards. As the leader reads each yellow card, the pupil with the green card that correctly completes the description reads it.

- For each title, group members turn over orange cards and describe what 'your best friend' says about the title.

B   Count the positive and negative reviews for each title and decide which ones your group is going to check out. Report to the class.

5 Write about yourself in your notebook.

- What famous place would you like to visit? Why?
- Talk about a film/show/album/game that a friend has recommended to you. What did he/she say about it?

All About Me   Date:_____

_____

_____

How Well Do I Know It Now?

6 Look at page 118 and your notebook. Draw again.

A   Use a different colour.

B   Read and think.

I can ask my teacher for help.

I can practise.

7 Rate this Checkpoint.

 very easy   easy   hard   very hard   fun   OK   not fun

Wordlist

Find these words in your language. Then write in your notebook.

Unit 1	Page	Unit 2	Page	Unit 3	Page
alternative	2	accomplishment	20	be upset with	27
assignment	6	ages	20	blame	33
be more careful	3	become a doctor	14	character	32
break	9	Braille	20	(cheat/don't cheat)	
ceremony	8	climb a mountain	14	in a test	26
curriculum	9	conflict resolution	21	deceive	33
daily	8	critical thinking	21	ethical behaviour	32
do homework	2	inventor	18	ethics	32
do it earlier	3	journalist	21	feel good about	
do it again	3	leader	21	(himself/herself)	27
end up	4	meet a world leader	14	feel guilty	26
finish a project	3	opera	20	get into trouble	26
free time	8	personal computing	20	pass on	33
hand in (an essay)	3	peace	21	proverb	33
homeschooling	5	play an instrument	14	qualities	32
licence	6	speak another language	14	regret	33
objective	9	start a company	14	(return/don't return)	
pace	9	symphony	20	a wallet	27
pay attention to the time	3	win a tournament	15	sayings	33
period	8	write and publish a book	14	(tell/don't tell) the truth	29
quality time	10			traits	32
stressful	4			treat	32
study for a test	3				
study period	8				
task	9				
timetable	2				
typical	8				
workshop	9				

Wordlist

Base Form	Past Simple	Base Form	Past Simple
become	became	meet	met
blame	blamed	pass	passed
bring	brought	pay	paid
cheat	cheated	play	played
climb	climbed	publish	published
compete	competed	read	read
cultivate	cultivated	regret	regretted
deceive	deceived	return	returned
digest	digested	run	ran
do	did	speak	spoke
download	downloaded	start	started
earn	earned	study	studied
estimate	estimated	tell	told
feel	felt	travel	travelled
finish	finished	treat	treated
fly	flew	turn	turned
get	got	tweet	tweeted
give	gave	upload	uploaded
hand	handed	win	won
have	had	work	worked
influence	influenced	write	wrote

Pearson Education Limited
Edinburgh Gate
Harlow
Essex CM20 2JE
England
and Associated Companies throughout the world.

www.pearsonelt.com/bigenglish

© Pearson Education Limited 2014

Authorised adaptation from the United States edition entitled Big English,
1st Edition, by Mario Herrera and Christopher Sol Cruz. Published by Pearson
Education Inc. © 2013 by Pearson Education, Inc.

The right of Mario Herrera and Christopher Sol Cruz to be identified as the
authors of this Work have been asserted by them in accordance with the
Copyright, Designs and Patents Act 1988.

First published 2014
Ninth impression 2018
ISBN: 978-1-4479-5131-5
Set in Apex Sans
Editorial and design management by Hyphen S.A.
Printed in Italy by L.E.G.O. S.p.A.

Acknowledgements

The publisher would like to thank the following for their contributions:

Tessa Lochowski for the stories and CLIL pages.

Sagrario Salaberri for the Phonics pages.

The publisher would like to thank the following for their kind permission to
reproduce photographs:

(Key: b-bottom; c-centre; l-left; r-right; t-top)

Alamy Images: Ace Stock Limited 58, Aflo Foto Agency 20b, Allstar Picture
Library 117, Anders Blomqvist 49cl, Andrew Woodley 113cl, Big Cheese Photo
LLC 67t, Blend Images 25cl, 49c, blickwinkel 84t, Cultura RM 23bc, 25bl, David
Pearson 89b, Design Pics Inc 2, dieKleinert 83tr, eddie linssen 23t, geogphotos
54tr, 78cr, GL Archive 20t, Glow Asia RF 4t, 5bc, 42br, 49cr, 76bl, 95br, Hemis
83tl, Ilya Genkin 94bc, Image Source 22, Image Source Plus 67br, Interfoto
112t, Jamie Pham Photography 107tc, Jeff Morgan 14 107tl, JHPhoto 112b,
Fredrick Kippe 106br, Megapress 49r, Michel Platini Fernandes Borges 4bc,
Mikko Mattila 9b, OJO Images Ltd 30, 110, PhotoAlto sas 4b, RGB Ventures LLC
dba SuperStock 20r, Marc Romanelli 98, RubberBall 27cl, Sabena Jane Blackbird
89t, 118tr, Sandra Baker, Science Photo Library 114t, Edd Westmacott 107tr;
Corbis: Citizen Stock / Blend Images 1cr, Randy Faris 66t, Image Source 70,
Rob Lewine / Tetra Images 1c, 1cl, Westend61 1r; **DK Images:** Linda Whitwam
82t; **Fotolia.com:** Alce 96, 97, AlienCat 82-83, amfroey01 17, 38bc, Andres
Rodriguez 44t, arekmalang 25br, 38c, biker3 4tc, bst2012 27c, caminoel 94b,
chawalitpix 60l, 78tr, DragonImages 53, ecco 94-95, Elenathewise 25t, Eric
Isselée 72t, faizzaki 72b, feferoni 83cl, Felix Mizioznikov 26r, 38t, Forever
115, gavran333 27r, 38bl, Goran Bogicevic 73t, gui yong nian 8t, Iva 94tl, J_Foto
27tl, Jogyx 14tr, Jörg Hackemann 63, 91b, Kalim 25cr, KaYann 94bl, lunamarina
64br, magann 21, Marta 14-15, Monteleone 5b, PiLensPhoto 83cr, 118br,
S.White 49l, Sabphoto 14br, sellingpix 43t, sjhuls 103b, Subbotina Anna 95cr,
vilainecrevette 77b, wenani 26-27; **Getty Images:** Barry King / WireImage 15cl,
Michael Wells 84-85, Sheldon Levis / Photolibrary 45, TAO Images Limited
23b, Vittorio Ricci - Italy / Flickr 84b; **Glow Images:** 88t, ImageBroker / Eckhard
Eibner 113b, Perspectives 14cr; **Newscom:** Ma Yan / Xinhua / Photoshot
15tl, Lucas Oleniuk 15tr; **Pearson Education:** Christopher Sol Cruz 16; **Press
Association Images:** Robert F. Bukaty 21b; **Rex Features:** View Pictures 44bl,
78br; **Shutterstock.com:** Aleksandar Todorovic 94tc, Aletia 95bl, Ann Worthy
55br, 107br, Anna Omelchenko 107cl, 118tc, antipathique 54-55, AVAVA 43br,
66l, bikeriderlondon 64bl, 111t, Blend Images, CandyBox Images 9, chungking
94tr, claudia veja 106bl, Costazzurra 54b, CREATISTA 55tc, Danomyte 62,
Dieter H 73bl, 113tl, Dudarev Mikhail 100b, Edyta Pawlowska 26l, egd 107cr,
erashov 111c, Fotohunter 101tl, Galina Barskaya 3cr, Gelpi JM 55bc, 107bl,
Giuseppe_R, Gurgen Bakhshetsyan 105, Holbox 27tc, Hubis 48t, Hugo Felix 108,
Hurst Photo 35, Iakov Filimonov, Intellistudies 47, irin-k 33, Jaimie Duplass 15bl,
104br, James Steidl 106bc, JaySi 59, Jenn Huls, John David Bigl III 77t, jsouthby
111b, julia 100t, 118bc, Julian Rovagnati 11, 101b, Junial Enterprises, Kamira
73l, karelnoppe 60b, KateStone, Kirill Saveliev 102, 118c, Kiselev Andrey
Valerevich 3b, kouptsova 4cl, 15br, 27br, 51r, 92br, Derek Latta 1l, Lisa F. Young
86t, Magdanatka 88, Matthew Jacques 94br, michaeljung 67bl, milias1987
32, Miriam Doerr 113tr, Monkey Business Images 18, 43bl, 51t, 66br, 114,
Nella 95tl, Neo Edmund 33c, Nestor Noci 95c, Odua Images 51b, Oleg_Mit 52,
Oleksiy Mark 42, 78b, Pamela Mullins 55cl, Pete Pahham 19, Phon Promwisate
95tr, photogl 14l, 38br, pippa west 101tr, Pius Lee 95cl, R. Gino Santa Maria

3cl, 5t, 116, Real Deal Photo 55tr, Rob Byron 27bl, Robert Crum 27tr, rudall30,
Sanmongkhol 92bl, Sergii Figurnyi 54l, Shane W Thompson 73br, silver-john
71, Slazdi 103t, Somchai Som 95tc, 118bl, Syda Productions 55bl, 83bl, szefei
93t, Tara Flake 4bl, 5tc, 76br, Tracy Whiteside 55tl, 55cr, 83br, Upthebanner 99,
wizdata 8, wow 91t, Zurijeta 51bl, 104bl; **SuperStock:** Somos 6

Cover images: *Front:* **Corbis:** Citizen Stock / Blend Images cr, Rob Lewine / Tetra
Images cl, c, Westend61 r; **Shutterstock.com:** Derek Latta l

All other images © Pearson Education

Every effort has been made to trace the copyright holders and we apologise
in advance for any unintentional omissions. We would be pleased to insert the
appropriate acknowledgement in any subsequent edition of this publication.

Illustrated by

Valentina Belloni, Paula Franco, Rob Sharp, Christos Skaltsas, Anthony Lewis.